W9-BFQ-724

The Complete
Geography
Project and
Activity Book

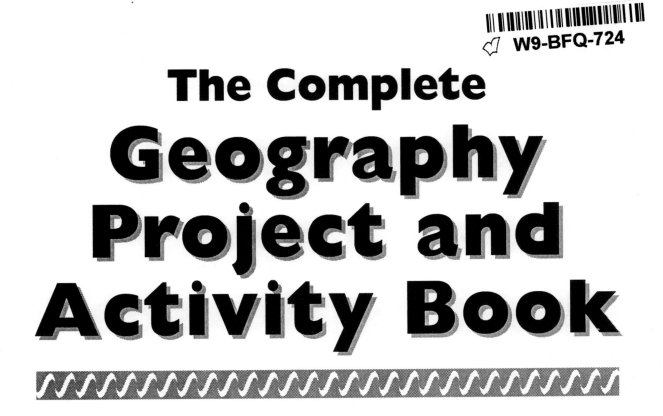

by

Susan Julio

SCHOLASTIC
PROFESSIONAL BOOKS

New York • Toronto • London • Auckland • Sydney

To Dale

Scholastic Inc. grants teacher permission to photocopy the activity sheets from this book for classroom use. No other part of this publication may be reproduced in whole or part, or stored in a retrieval system, or transmitted in any form or by any means, electronic, mechanical, photocopying, recording or otherwise, without written permission of the publisher. For permission, write to Scholastic Professional Books, 555 Broadway, New York, NY 10012-3999.

Book design by Nancy Metcalf, Intergraphics
Book illustrations by Lynn Vinyard
Cover design by Vincent Ceci
Cover illustration by Mona Mark

ISBN 0-590-49473-2

Copyright © 1993 by Susan Julio.
All rights reserved.
Printed in the U.S.A.

Table of Contents

Introduction

The Earth is truly amazing! The third planet from the Sun in our Solar System provides the perfect conditions for life. On Earth, we have the right temperatures, the right mixture of atmospheric gases, and the proper food sources to provide for the sustainment of the human race.

Geography, by definition, explores the different ways that the surface of the Earth is affected by nature and changed by human uses. The ideas presented in this book are designed to bring geography to life for your students. The activities will involve them in discovering and responding to the abundant resources found on the Earth.

About This Book

The main contents consist of 20 lessons that are planned to form a developmental sequence. You may, of course, omit lessons or change their order to suit your particular classroom needs.

Following the lessons there are nine bulletin board projects related to various lesson concepts. See pages 81–107 for further details.

How to Use This Book

Although the lessons can easily be adapted to a traditional classroom setting, they are designed to be used in a cooperative learning environment. A cooperative learning strategy develops the academic and social skills of students by allowing them to learn from one another. The teacher's role is one of facilitator, encouraging students to take risks and share what they feel as well as what they know.

Building Cooperative Groups

The lessons in this book incorporate four types of groups:
1. Whole Class.
2. Large Group—the class divided into halves or thirds.
3. Small Group—made up of 4–6 members.
4. Partners—members of small groups divided into pairs.

Small groups are suggested for most of the activities in this book. In group work, every student is responsible for contributing to the common effort. Small groups, especially, cannot successfully complete an activity without every member's involvement. When you form your groups, therefore, it is a good idea to select a variety of differing personality types and ability levels. Working together as a team teaches students the importance of cooperation. In addition, students develop self-confidence as they discover that they can accomplish things in groups that would have been beyond them working alone. As they interact, they help one another to learn.

Group Jobs

When students work in small groups, it helps to have a specific job assigned to each member. As a reminder, each child should be given a job title along with a job name tag. (See the reproducible tags on page 6.) Since jobs will be rotated from lesson to lesson, take the time to make students aware of the responsibilities of each position. Stress that each job is equally important.

For groups of six, the jobs and their responsibilities are:

Director:
Leads group discussions and ensures directions are followed and assignments completed.

Secretary:
Distributes and collects work materials and assignments. Records group ideas.

Spokesperson:
Reports group needs and concerns to the teacher. Gives oral reports as required.

Monitor:
Maintains orderliness and quietness of group members. Directs cleanup.

Facilitator:
Mediates disagreements between group members and works to see that opinions are openly expressed and respected by others.

Booster:
Encourages members with words of praise and positive comments.

For groups of four, the jobs of Monitor, Facilitator, and Booster can be combined.

You should provide each small group with a folder to contain work in progress and completed assignments. Store the folders in an easily accessible location.

In most cooperative learning situations, grades are assigned to groups rather than to the individual members. This grading method encourages members to work together. While the children are working, the teacher should circulate throughout the room, observing, answering, and prompting students. It is essential to check on how well groups are functioning and whether members are performing their roles effectively. Do not hesitate to make changes in group membership when problems occur.

Classroom Reference Library

Reference materials play an important part in many of the activities in this book. Most school media centers are helpful in providing teachers with a wide assortment of materials to use in the classroom on a temporary basis. When assembling your in-class library, be sure to include dictionaries, atlases, almanacs, encyclopedias, magazines, nonfiction books, textbooks (old and new), computer programs, films, filmstrips, videos, flashcards, posters, records, and tapes. Display the materials in the classroom and provide instruction (as necessary) in the proper use of these resources.

Job Name Tags

Reproduce a set of the name tags (page 6) for each small group. Place each badge inside a clear plastic name tag holder (available from office supply stores). Keep the badges in zipper plastic bags when not in use.

Job Name Tags

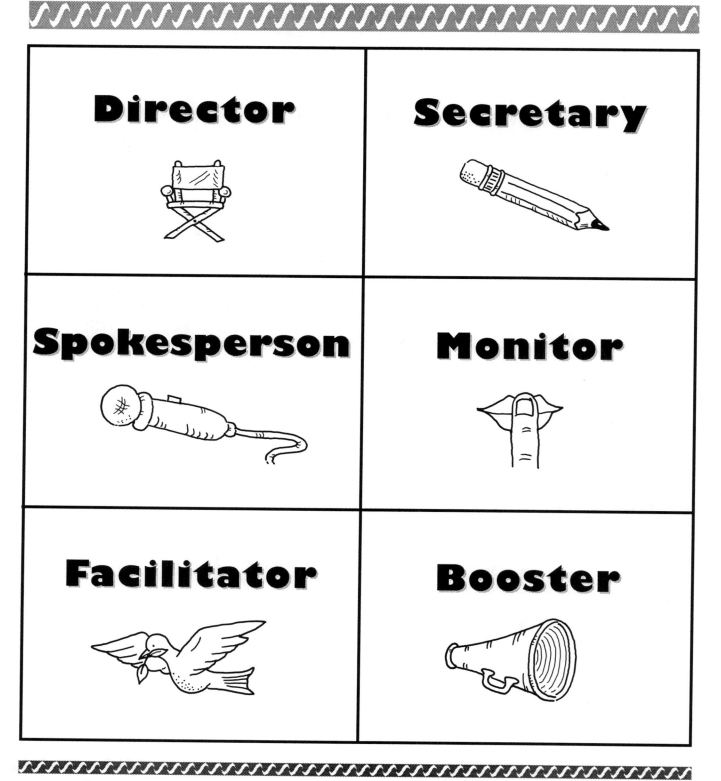

Director

Secretary

Spokesperson

Monitor

Facilitator

Booster

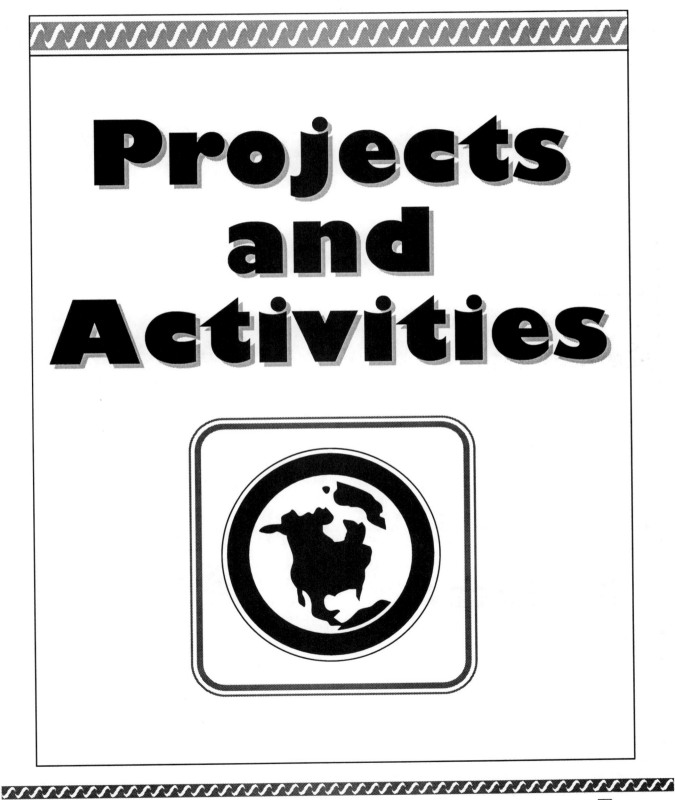

Projects and Activities

Space Travelers

Objective:
Students will learn how to define geography and discuss its various aspects.

Background

Geography is the study of features on the Earth's surface. These include land and water formations, climate, soil types, plant and animal and human life, and human uses and divisions of the land.

Materials

1. A dictionary.

For each group:

2. Large pieces of construction paper
3. Glue.

For each student:

4. Crayon or marker.
5. One 5 x 8-inch piece of construction paper.
6. A copy of the Intergalactic Passport (page 10).

Preparation

Cut large sheets of construction paper (one for each group) into a pennant shape. Organize students into small groups.

Activity

Begin the lesson by writing the word *geography* on the board. Select a student to locate the word in the dictionary and then read the entry aloud to the class. Copy the definition on the board. Highlight any words that may not be familiar. Rewrite the definition if necessary, making sure every student understands it.

Explain to the class that each group is going on a special mission. As explorers from another planet, they have been sent to study the Planet Earth and learn all they can about it—a sort of intergalactic field trip! Before beginning their voyage, each group must work together to decide on a name for its planet (either real or imaginary) and design a space pennant. Each pennant should have the planet name on the front, and on the back, a list of at least five questions that each group would like answered about the Planet Earth.

Distribute the pre-cut pennants and markers. Provide students time to complete the assignment. When each group is finished, have the group spokespersons take turns presenting their group pennants. Then hang the pennants in the classroom.

Extension

Invite the students to create an "Intergalactic Passport." Each child should make up a space alias and write a "mission statement" (something they particularly want to study about Earth) in the passport. They then cut out the two sections and glue them to the front and inside of a 5 x 8-inch piece of construction paper folded in half. Post the passports in the room and have the students guess who made each passport.

Intergalactic Passport

1. In the box, draw a picture of yourself as a visitor from another planet.
2. Write your alien name, DOB (Date of Birth), and planet name on the next lines.
3. After "Mission," write a sentence or two describing what you hope to learn about Planet Earth.
4. Fold a piece of construction paper in half. Cut out the cover of the Passport and glue it to the outside of the folded paper. Cut out the identification part of the Passport and glue it to the inside of the paper.

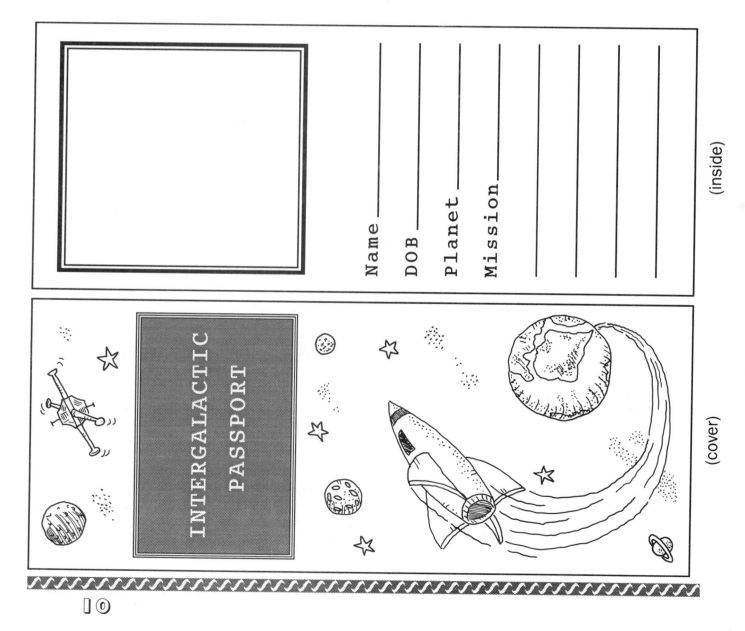

Name

DOB

Planet

Mission

(inside)

INTERGALACTIC PASSPORT

(cover)

Planet Earth

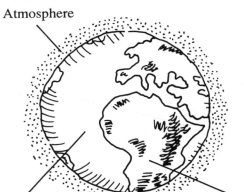

Objective:
Students will explore some of the Earth's unique characteristics.

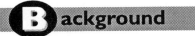ackground

The Earth is one of nine planets that revolve around the Sun. It is the fifth largest planet (7,918 miles average diameter) and is composed of rock, metal, water, and air. Water covers about 71 percent of the Earth's surface. The atmosphere is made up of a mixture of gases, including carbon dioxide, nitrogen, and oxygen. The Earth is the only planet in our Solar System that is known to support life.

aterials

1. Photo of Earth from space (optional).
2. Shoe box.
3. Black construction paper (enough to cover the shoe box).

For each group:

4. Reference materials.
5. Scissors.
6. Stapler.
7. Crayons.

For each student:

8. A copy of the What's Outside? worksheet (page 13).
9. A copy of the Earth Riddle booklet (page 14).

reparation

Obtain enough reference materials for each small group. Make a copy of the What's Outside? worksheet and Earth Riddle booklet for each student. For the extension, use a stapler to cover the shoe box with black paper, and cut a small slit in the center of the lid.

Activity

To start the activity, sketch the following diagram on the board.

Atmosphere

Water   Land

PLANET EARTH

Ask students to assume their space alias again and imagine they are in a spaceship headed toward Earth. They are looking at the Earth from the spaceship window. (Display the space photo of Earth, if you have it.) What do they see? Generate responses such as swirling gases, water, and land. Label each part of the chalk diagram as it is mentioned.

Distribute the What's Outside? worksheet and allow students to complete it, using the chalkboard diagram as a model. (Group secretaries should collect the finished diagrams and store them in the group folders.)

Next, give each student an Earth Riddle booklet. Guide the students as they assemble the booklets by cutting out the pages, putting them in order, and stapling the edges together. Read the riddles together and then have the students research the answers in groups. Review and discuss the booklet when all the groups have finished.

Answers to the Earth Riddle booklet:
1. Earth
2. water
3. granite
4. nitrogen

Extension

Invite the students to create their own Earth riddles throughout the unit. Write them (and the answers) on a slip of paper and put them in the prepared shoe box. During any spare minutes, take some riddles from the box and have students guess the answers.

What's Outside?

Label, color, and cut out along the dotted line.

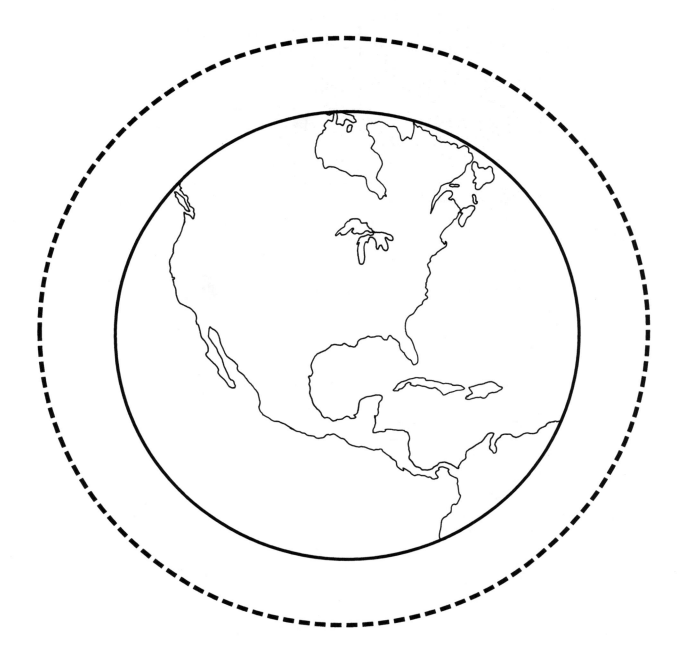

Earth Riddles

Venus is in front of me, Mars is behind me. Who am I?

I cover most of the Earth's surface. Who am I?

I am the rock that makes up most of the land. What kind of rock am I?

Our atmosphere is mostly made up of oxygen and me. What gas am I?

Inside Out

Objective:
Students will identify the different layers that make up the Earth.

Background

A cross-section of the Earth reveals the following sections:

Atmosphere: These are the gases that surround the Earth, They are dense at the surface but thin out to almost nothing at an altitude of 15 miles.

Crust: This is the outer portion of the Earth. Consisting largely of solid rock, it is approximately 22 miles deep under land and 6 miles deep under the ocean.

Mantle: This hot layer of rock extends downward about 1,800 miles. Part of the mantle near the crust is molten.

Outer Core: This consists of hot liquid metal, mostly iron and nickel. It is approximately 2,160 miles deep.

Inner Core: Composed of very hot solid metal, this is approximately 780 miles in diameter.

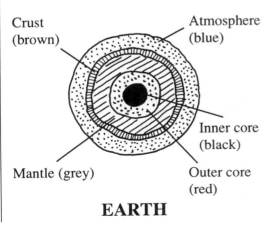

Crust (brown)
Atmosphere (blue)
Inner core (black)
Mantle (grey)
Outer core (red)

EARTH

Materials

1. Colored chalk.
2. Baker's clay (see Preparation).
3. Red plasticene or nonhardening clay (see Preparation).
4. Access to an oven.

For each group:

5. Scissors.
6. A hole punch.

For each student:

7. One 3 x 5-inch index card.
8. Crayons.
9. Two 2-foot lengths of yarn.
10. One dozen small pebbles.
11. A copy of the What's Inside? worksheet (page 17).
12. One 1/4-inch ball bearing.
13. One small paper clip.
14. Green and blue enamel or acrylic paint.
15. A paint brush.

Preparation

To make baker's clay, you need:
• 1 cup of salt
• 1 1/4 cups of warm water
• 4 cups of flour
   Place the salt in a bowl, add the warm water, and stir. Slowly add the flour and knead the mixture for 10 minutes. Bake at 325°F for 1 hour. Let cool.
   To make red nonhardening clay, you need:
• 2 cups of flour
• 1/2 cup of salt
• 4 tablespoons of salad oil
• 8 tablespoons of water
• A few drops of red food coloring

Mix all the ingredients in a large bowl and knead to a clay-like consistency.

Just before the lesson, copy the diagram on page 15 on the board using colored chalk.

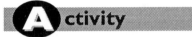

Activity

Begin with a class discussion of the sections of the Earth. Point out that most of these sections are always moving. Explain that students will create a "living Earth" to demonstrate how the Earth moves. Divide students up as follows:
• 7 or 8 students to portray the atmosphere;
• 9 or 10 students to portray the crust;
• 7 or 8 students to portray the mantle;
• 3 or 4 students to portray the outer core;
• 1 student to portray the inner core.

Using index cards, crayons, hole punch, and yarn, children can make tags (labeled with their layer names) to wear around their necks. Inform the students that when you give a signal (such as blowing a whistle) they will perform actions in accordance with the section of the Earth they are portraying. Move to a clear area and arrange students as follows:
• *Inner Core:* This student stands in the middle. At the signal, the inner core flexes his/her muscles and chants "Inner core."
• *Outer Core:* Students join hands, facing inward, surrounding the inner core. At the signal, they walk clockwise (to show that this portion of the Earth is liquid) and chant "Outer core."
• *Mantle:* Students join hands, facing outward, and surround the outer core. At the signal, they walk counterclockwise while raising and lowering their arms to show the

movement in this part of the Earth. They chant "Mantle."
• *Crust:* These students join hands around the mantle, facing outward. At the signal, they remain still (the surface of the Earth doesn't move much unless there is an earthquake) and chant "Crust."
• *Atmosphere:* Students are positioned at intervals around the crust. At the signal, they spin and twirl (to show the lightness and mobility of air) while chanting "Atmosphere."

When everyone is in position, count to three, give the signal, and watch the Earth come alive!

Reassemble students into their original groups and make sure they have their completed What's Outside? worksheets from the previous lesson. Have them complete the What's Inside? worksheet and then attach it to the What's Outside? worksheet to make a fold-away diagram.

Extension

Give each student a ball bearing, a blob of red nonhardening clay (or plasticene), a blob of baker's clay, a dozen small pebbles, a paper clip, and a length of yarn. Ask the students to recreate a mini-Earth, using the diagram of the Earth's cross-section as a guide.

Beginning with the ball bearing as the inner core, students should form the red nonhardening clay around it as the outer core. Next, they embed the pebbles around the outside to serve as the mantle. Finally, they roll the entire ball in baker's clay and insert a paper clip approximately 3/4 of the way into the ball.

Bake the mini-Earths. When they are cool, have students paint them with Earth colors. Then, when they are dry, students insert the yarn through the paper clip and the Earth pendant is ready to wear!

What's Inside?

Label, color, and cut out the picture below. Fold the picture along the dotted line in the middle. Flatten the picture out. Carefully place glue along the dotted lines marked "glue."

Now take the What's Outside? picture you prepared earlier. Place it on top of the What's Inside? picture and press down. You can now fold down the flap below to see inside the Earth.

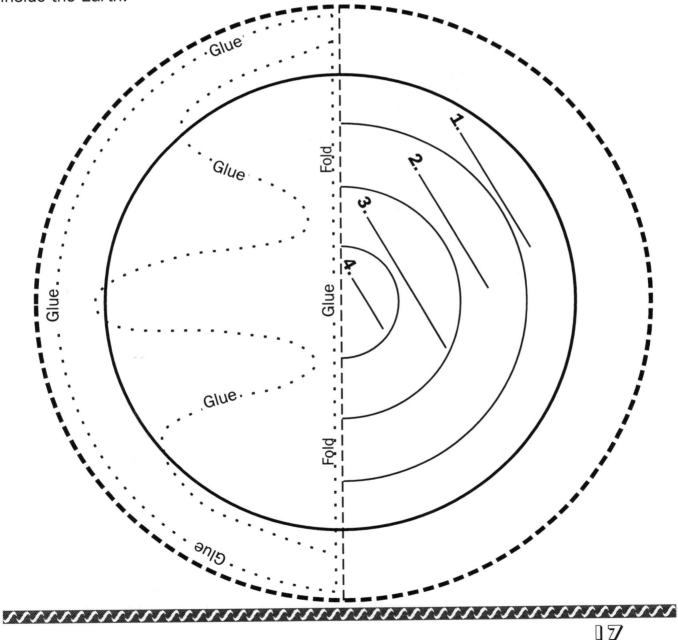

Natural Wonders

Objective:
Students will distinguish between land and water forms and identify examples of each.

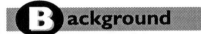 Background

The surface of the Earth is covered with a remarkable variety of land and water features. Water is more abundant than land. Oceans, seas, lakes, and rivers cover a large part of the Earth's surface and surround the mountains, peninsulas, and other formations found on land.

Materials

1. A sheet of chart paper.
2. A marker.
3. Postcards (see Preparation).

For each pair:

4. A set of Picture/Definition cards (pages 19 and 20).

For each student:

5. A My Strange Adventure worksheet (pages 21 and 22).

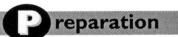 Preparation

Well ahead of time, ask the students to bring in any postcards they have collected or received in the mail.

Divide the students into small groups, but have them work in pairs for most of this unit. Copy and cut out a set of Picture/Definition cards for each pair.

Copy the rebus story worksheet for each student. Divide a sheet of chart paper into two sections labeled "Land" and "Water."

Activity

Ask those students with postcards to share them with the class. Direct the students' attention to the land and/or water forms they see on each card. List these features on the chart paper, along with others the children are familiar with.

Next, give each pair a set of Picture/Definition cards. Have one partner read the definition card and the other partner match it with the correct picture. Help with any terms that students may not understand, such as *body* of water or land. Check all completed matches. Add to the chart paper list any new land or water features discovered.

Finally, distribute the My Strange Adventure worksheet for each student to complete. (Students may refer to their Picture/Definition cards for assistance.) Group secretaries should collect the finished stories.

Extensions

• Assemble all of the stories and bind them into a classroom book. Keep the book in the classroom library for students to read and enjoy.

• Use the Feature Presentation Bulletin Board on page 88 to round out this activity.

Picture Cards

Definition Cards

Bay A body of water that extends into the land.	**Gulf** Part of an ocean or sea partly enclosed by land.	**Valley** A long hollow between hills or mountains.
Mesa A rise of land having a flat top and steep walls.	**Island** A body of land that is surrounded by water on all sides.	**Mountain** A large elevation of the Earth's surface.
Volcano A vent or crack in the Earth's surface through which molten rock escapes.	**River** A stream of water of a large size.	**Waterfall** A fall or flow of water from above.
Peninsula A body of land that is surrounded by water on three of it's sides.	**Strait** A narrow flow of water that connects two bigger bodies of water.	**Lake** A large body of water completely surrounded by land.

My Strange Adventure

Complete this story by drawing a picture of a *thing* in every ◯ , a *land form* in every ▢ , a *water form* in every ◇ , and a *creature* in every △ .

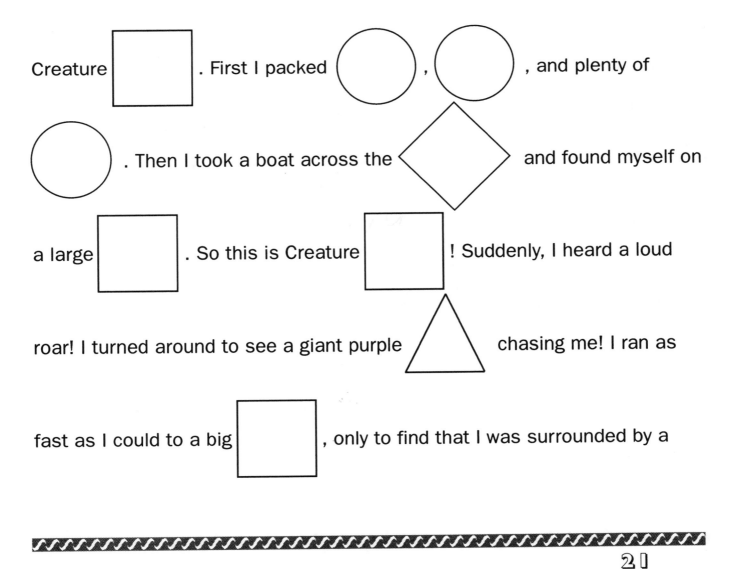

One morning I woke up bright and early and decided to take a trip to

Creature ▢ . First I packed ◯ , ◯ , and plenty of

◯ . Then I took a boat across the ◇ and found myself on

a large ▢ . So this is Creature ▢ ! Suddenly, I heard a loud

roar! I turned around to see a giant purple △ chasing me! I ran as

fast as I could to a big ▢ , only to find that I was surrounded by a

Name ______________________________

My Strange Adventure (cont.)

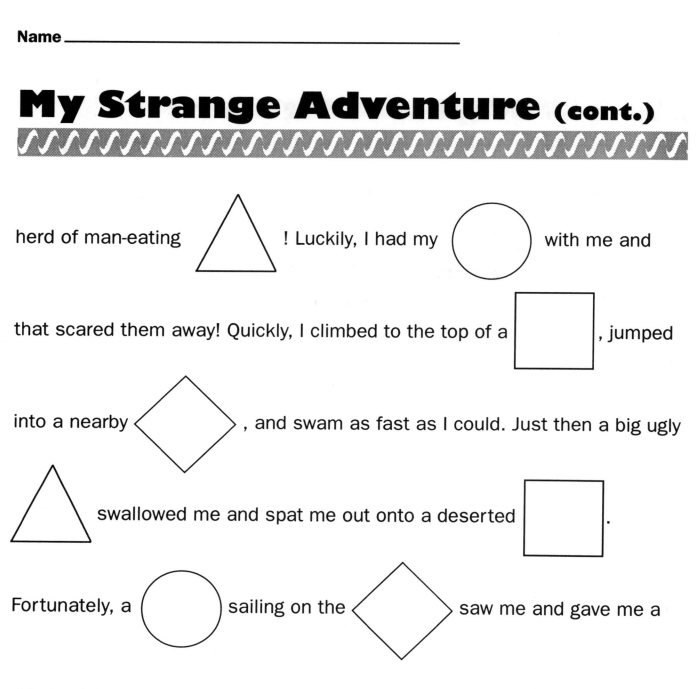

herd of man-eating △ ! Luckily, I had my ○ with me and that scared them away! Quickly, I climbed to the top of a □ , jumped into a nearby ◇ , and swam as fast as I could. Just then a big ugly △ swallowed me and spat me out onto a deserted □ . Fortunately, a ○ sailing on the ◇ saw me and gave me a ride back home. Whew! What a trip!

People's Touch

Objective:
Students will be able to discuss different ways in which humans have changed their environment.

Background

A closer examination of the Earth's surface shows that land and water formations aren't the only distinguishable features. Humans have added, in ever increasing numbers, vast networks of transportation routes, urban centers, factories, bridges, tunnels, and dwellings of every kind. These are evidence of the ability of humans to change their environment to suit their needs.

For as long as humans have existed, they have been adapting the Earth and its resources. Some of the changes have been good for the environment, while others have had detrimental effects.

Materials

1. Reference materials.
2. Recyclable materials for building: boxes, cans, containers, etc. (see Preparation).

For each group:

3. A sheet of bulletin board paper.
4. Poster paints and brushes.
5. Scissors.
6. Glue.
7. Adhesive tape.
8. Crayons.
9. A large sheet of light-colored construction paper.

Preparation

Start early enough to collect sufficient amounts of building material for each small group. Keep the gathered materials in a large box or bag.

Cut a 2-foot-long piece of bulletin board paper for each group.

Activity

Begin by asking your students to imagine that they are back on their spaceships. Remind them of how they first saw the Earth through its swirling atmosphere and how the land and water features slowly came into sight. Review the types of formations they were able to see as the ship came closer to the Earth. Tell the class that it is now time to land and investigate further.

As the spaceship door begins to open, what other things do they see? Direct student responses to human-made features such as buildings, roads, and bridges, and share some of the pictures in the reference books that show cities or towns. Help students distinguish between urban and rural areas by pointing out differences in the way the land is used and in the types of buildings and transportation. Discuss how some places are full of buildings and people while other places are mostly stretches of land. Talk about which features may be beneficial or detrimental to our environment.

Next, direct student attention to the bulletin board paper and building materials. Invite each group to work out a plan for building a landscape on its piece of bulletin board paper. (Group secretaries will choose the building materials for their groups.) Each group must decide what types of land and water features they will have, as well as which areas will become urban and which rural. Groups must agree on who will be responsible for "developing" each area and then begin building.

Extension

When the landscapes are finished, provide each group with a large sheet of construction paper. Have them make a map of their area. Encourage them to give names to appropriate items or places of interest. Assemble the maps for a classroom atlas.

Natural Changers

Objective:
Students will explore the ways in which natural forces change the Earth's surface.

Background

The surface of the Earth is constantly changing. Over the course of time, natural forces such as wind, water, and ice slowly alter the appearance of the Earth. These forces wear away some areas while building up others. This process can be divided into three parts:

1. *Weathering:* The eroding or breaking down of the Earth's surface by wind, water, ice, chemicals, or heat.
2. *Transportation:* The removal of the weathered material.
3. *Deposition:* The accumulation of the transported material.

In this lesson, students will explore and observe the ways in which the forces of nature change the Earth.

Materials

1. Plenty of newspapers.

For Station 1 (see Preparation):

2. Rectangular cake pan.
3. Soil.
4. Small stones.
5. A sprinkler-type watering can.

For Station 2:

6. Shallow cardboard box.
7. Sand.
8. Small rock.
9. Enough straws for each student to have one.

For Station 3:

10. A large ice-cube tray.
11. Soil.
12. Pebbles.
13. Small insulated cooler.
14. Rectangular piece of wood covered with waxed paper.
15. Blocks or books for support.
16. Two hand-held hair dryers.

For Station 4:

17. Mixing bowl.
18. Large spoon.
19. A measuring cup and measuring spoons.
20. Knife.
21. An 8 x 8-inch cake pan.
22. Large pot.
23. Potholder.
24. Aluminum foil.
25. Hot plate.
26. Recipe ingredients (see the worksheet on page 30).
27. Paper towels.
28. Pot scrubber pad.
29. Dish detergent.

For each student:

30. A copy of the Natural Changers worksheet (pages 27–30).

Preparation

This activity involves the use of four stations or work areas. A station can be any large surface—a table, a section of the floor, or whatever space is available. Cover each station's surface with newspaper. Then label and set up the four stations as follows:

1. Water as a Changer

Mix the soil with some sand and stones and form a mound in the middle of the cake pan. Fill the watering can with water and place it nearby.

2. Wind as a Changer

Fill the box with approximately 2 inches of sand. Beside it place the stone and straws.

3. Ice as a Changer

Prepare these "glacier" ice cubes beforehand:

a. Fill the ice-cube tray 1/4 full of water. Freeze.

b. Remove the tray from the freezer and add 1/4 inch of soil. Freeze.

c. Remove and add 1/4 inch of small pebbles. Freeze.

d. Remove and top with more water. Freeze.

Keep the cubes in the cooler until ready to use. Set one end of the waxed-paper-covered board on blocks or books to make a 6-inch-high incline. Have the hair dryers available nearby.

4. Glacier Bars

Set out all the cooking utensils and enough ingredients for four groups. Keep the detergent, pot scrubber, and paper towels by a sink.

Reproduce the Natural Changers worksheet for each student. Divide the class into four large groups labeled A, B, C, and D and copy the following rotation chart on the chalkboard:

Group	1	2	3	4
A	Water	Wind	Ice	Cooking
B	Wind	Ice	Cooking	Water
C	Ice	Cooking	Water	Wind
D	Cooking	Water	Wind	Ice

Activity

Begin by asking students to think about the various ways that nature changes the Earth. Write the word "weathering" on the board. Help the students understand that this term refers to the ways in which soil, rock, and sand can be removed from one place and added to another.

Distribute the Natural Changers worksheets and explain to the class that they will be visiting several work stations that will help them learn more about the process of weathering. Instruct the students to fill out their worksheets at each station. Point out the station locations and call attention to the rotation chart on the board. Remind the students that at the Glacier Bars. station you are the only person who should operate the hot plate.

At an agreed upon signal (such as a whistle blow) each group will move to a station, where they will work for 15 minutes. Each time the signal is repeated, groups switch to another station until all stations have been completed. During each work period, provide a five-minute warning to alert the students to start wrapping things up.

Extension

Go over the Natural Changers worksheets (pages 27–30) together in class, while enjoying the Glacier Bars made at Station 4.

Name _____

Station 1:
Water as a Changer

Water is one of the natural elements that change our Earth. In fact, moving water is the Earth's greatest changer. How does water do that? Let's find out!

The pan in front of you contains a small mountain of soil, sand, and pebbles. Take turns holding the watering can over the mountain. (Make sure everyone in the group gets a chance to water.) Imagine you are making a rainstorm. Observe what happens and answer these questions:

1. How did the mountain look before the rainstorm? Illustrate your answer.

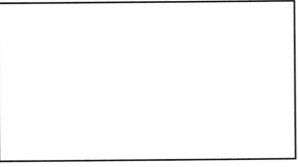

2. How did the mountain look after the rainstorm? Illustrate your answer.

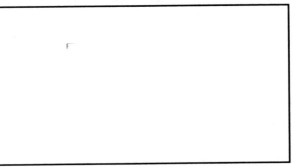

3. What did the water remove from the mountain? (This is called *weathering.*)

_____

4. How did the "rain" carry off the bits of soil, sand, and stone? (This is called *transportation*.) _____

5. Where did the removed pieces end up? (This is called *deposition.)*

_____

6. Rain is one way water acts as a changer. Rivers and streams are other ways. Did you see any little rivers form on the mountain during the rainstorm? _____

If yes, what changes happened because of the rivers?_____

_____

Water acts as a changer by washing and carrying away soil and bits of rock, and depositing it in other places.

Cleanup: Rebuild the mountain in the middle of the pan for the next group. Wash your hands and refill the watering can at the sink.

Name _____

Station 2: Wind as a Changer

Wind is another of the natural elements that change our Earth. Wind can act as a changer by blowing small particles of rock and sand against an object until part of it wears away. Also, wind can blow sand into hills or ridges called *dunes*. You can see these in deserts and on beaches.

Often the shape of a dune can show the direction the wind is blowing. The three most common dune shapes are shown below. Using clean straws, take turns recreating them. Blow very gently in the direction of the arrows.

Transverse dunes have small ridges that form lines in the direction of the wind.

Crescent dunes are built up around *obstructions*. (An obstruction is something that gets in the way.) Put the stone in the box before gently blowing the sand. **Note:** The crescent tips point in the direction of the wind.

Star dunes are formed when wind comes from different directions.

What other shapes can you make by gentle blowing? Now answer these questions:

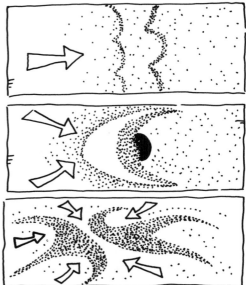

1. How did the dunes change shape? (This is called *weathering*.)

_____

2. How did sand move from one dune to another? (This is called *transportation*.)

_____

3. Where did the removed pieces end up? (This is called *deposition*.)

_____

4. What are some other things the wind can carry?

_____

Wind shapes the land by wearing away rock and carrying loose pieces from one place to another.

Cleanup: Smooth out the sand and throw away the used straws.

Station 3:
Ice as a Changer

When water becomes hard and solid, it is called ice. Ice can change the Earth in many ways. Water in soil or between rocks can make cracks as it freezes.

In cold and mountainous areas there are slow-moving rivers of ice called *glaciers*. As a glacier moves downhill, parts of it melt and refreeze, so it can pick up rocks and soil from one place and leave them in other places. Glaciers can also scrape the land they travel over, leaving deep valleys behind.

Let's take a closer look at glaciers. With other group members, take 2 or 3 glacier cubes from the cooler. Place the cubes at the top of the board. Use a hair dryer to melt the cubes so they travel downhill. When the cubes have melted, answer these questions:

1. What was the glacier made of?_____

2. In a real glacier, where would the soil and rock come from? (This is called *weathering*.) _____

3. How did the bits of soil and stone move? (This is called *transportation*.)

_____

4. What did the glacier leave behind as it melted? (This is called *deposition*.)

_____

5. How does a glacier change the Earth?

_____

Water that freezes and moves acts as a changer by picking up soil and rock from one place and leaving it in another place when it melts.

Cleanup: Wipe the board clean with paper towels. Make sure the hair dryers are turned off.

Station 4: Glacier Bars

Take time out for a special treat! Carefully read the following recipe, and then start work on the ingredients. Make sure everyone in the group gets a turn measuring and mixing.

Ingredients:

- 1 cup of tiny marshmallows
- 1 teaspoon of margarine
- 1/8 teaspoon of vanilla
- 2 cups of rice cereal
- 1/2 cup of chocolate chips
- 1/4 cup of chopped nuts

Directions:

1. Wash your hands.
2. Line the pan with aluminum foil. Use your fingers to rub 1/2 teaspoon of margarine onto the foil.
3. Have your teacher turn on the hot plate to medium. Remember to always use a potholder when removing a pot from the burner!
4. Put the marshmallows and 1/2 teaspoon of margarine into the pot. Stir constantly until the marshmallows are melted. Remove the pot from the heat using a potholder. Turn the hot plate to "Off."
5. Stir in the vanilla and the cereal.
6. Put half of the mixture into the pan, pressing down evenly with the spoon. Pretend this is the snow and ice part of the glacier.
7. Sprinkle the chocolate chips on top. This is the soil part of the glacier.
8. Put the rest of the marshmallow mixture in the pan and press firmly down.
9. Sprinkle the chopped nuts on top. These are bits of rock and stone in the glacier.
10. Carefully remove the foil and glacier from the pan. Set it aside to cool. Ask your teacher to cut it into bars when it cools off.

Cleanup: Wipe up any spills with a paper towel. Use the detergent and scrubbing pad to clean the dishes at the sink.

Movers and Shakers

Objective:
Students will be able to identify major natural disasters and describe how they affect the Earth.

ackground

Nature's gentler elements change the environment over a long period of time. There are more violent natural forces, such as earthquakes, volcanic eruptions, tornadoes, hurricanes, floods, and tidal waves that can create devastating changes in a matter of seconds. In addition, drought can change an environment drastically in a matter of weeks. This lesson will focus on several of these more violent occurrences:

1. Earthquakes:
These happen somewhere in the world every day. While most earthquakes are so small they can't be felt, others are strong enough to cause great destruction and loss of life. Earthquakes occur when sections of the Earth's crust (called plates) press against each other and then slip. When an earthquake happens under an ocean, it may cause a *tsunami* (often called a tidal wave).

2. Volcanoes:
A volcano is a hole or crack in the surface of the Earth that allows the hot, liquid rock and the gases formed in the mantle to escape. Some volcanoes erupt suddenly, spilling lava (liquid rock) over a large area. Others erupt more quietly, with little noise.

3. Drought:
A drought is a long period of rainless weather that causes river beds to dry up and large cracks to form in the soil.

4. Tornadoes and Hurricanes:
Tornadoes and hurricanes are violent wind storms. A tornado (or twister) consists of a tall, funnel-shaped mass of spinning air that contains moisture and debris. It rotates at over 200 miles per hour and moves across the land at speeds up to 60 miles per hour.

Hurricanes (also called typhoons and cyclones) begin over warm ocean waters. Moisture in the air rises and twists upwards, creating a suction in the eye or middle. Once on land, hurricanes begin to lose their strength.

5. Floods:
Heavy rainfall can cause bodies of water to overflow and spread onto land. Soil, plants, roads, and buildings can all be washed away and destroyed during a flood.

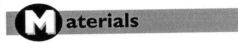aterials

1. Reference materials.
2. A tape recorder (or, if available, one for each group).
3. Blank tape cassettes.

For each group:

4. A copy of the Disaster News Network radio script (pages 33 and 34).

reparation

Find pictures in the reference books that show examples of natural disasters.

Mark these pages. Plan to arrange the class into groups of ten.

Activity

Begin the lesson by showing the pictures of natural disasters you have marked, and draw a Natural Disaster web (like the one below) on the chalkboard. Encourage students to fill in each circle with the name of a disaster and words describing what it is and does.

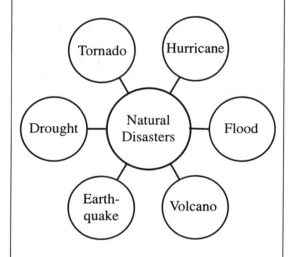

Ask students to relate any first-hand experiences of a natural disaster. Discuss the difference between disasters caused by forces of nature and those caused by humans (such as dropping a lighted match in a forest).

Invite students to look more closely at natural disasters by taking part in a "radio" play. Distribute copies of the Disaster News Network (DNN) radio script to all students and assign them to groups. Ask the students to choose parts and rehearse the play several times.

When the groups are ready, have them record the play using a tape recorder and a blank cassette. Play back the tapes later and enjoy the broadcasts! (You may even be creative and add appropriate sound effects.)

As an alternative, you might convert the play to a telecast, using a video camera, charts, graphs, and other props.

Extension

Ask the students to find and clip news of natural disasters from newspapers and magazines. Use these clippings to create a montage of natural disasters.

Disaster News Network (DNN)
(A Radio Play)

CAST

Ava Lanche (Head Anchor)

Hal Storm (Weather Reporter)

Ty Foon (World Correspondent)

Rock Slyde (Sports Reporter)

Dr. Fault (Earthquake Scientist)

Sue Nami (Travel Correspondent)

Sy Clone (Local News Reporter)

Farmer Famine (A Farmer)

Commercial Announcer

Tape Recorder Operator

*The **Tape Recorder Operator** begins recording and silently counts to three. At the count of three, begin....*

Ava Lanche: Good evening and welcome to DNN, Disaster News Network. In our top story today, we go live to the small country of Tremorland. Our World Correspondent, Ty Foon, is there and will give us some earth shaking news. Ty?

Ty Foon: Thank you, Ava. Here in the remote countryside of Tremorland, the residents are quite shook up. At 8 o'clock this morning a small earthquake caused many buildings to collapse and injured several people. I have with me Dr. S. Andreas Fault, a leading expert on earthquakes. Dr. Fault, what can you tell us?

Dr. Fault: Well, Ty, according to my *seismograph* [SIZE-moh-graf], this earthquake was a three on the *Richter* [RIK-ter] *scale*.

Ty Foon: What does all that mean, Doctor?

Dr. Fault: Well, Ty, a seismograph is a machine that we scientists use to record and measure the movements an earthquake makes. A Richter scale tells us the strength of the earthquake. A one on the Richter scale would be a very weak earthquake and a ten would be a very powerful one. The earthquake that hit Tremorland this morning was a three.

Ty Foon: Dr. Fault can you tell us how this happened?

Dr. Fault: Certainly. The Earth's crust is divided into large pieces called plates. These plates float on the melted rock in the mantle, so they move about very slowly. When they slip up or down or alongside one another, they cause the land above to shake.

Ty Foon: Is that what happened here?

Dr. Fault: Of course! But luckily it was a fairly weak earthquake. More powerful ones do a lot more damage. They can leave huge cracks in the ground. And earthquakes under the ocean can cause huge waves called *tsunami* [soo-NAH-mee].

Ty Foon: Thank you, Doctor. Back to you, Ava.

Ava Lanche: Thanks, Ty. On the local front, farmers here have been asking for help with a different problem. Local reporter Sy Clone has more on the story. Sy?

(Sound effects: farm noises.)

Sy Clone: Thanks, Ava. I'm here with one of our local farmers, Farmer Famine. Farmer Famine, why are you and other farmers angry?

Farmer Famine: Well, Mr. Clone, it's this here drought.

Sy Clone: Drought?

Farmer Famine: Yup. You know, a drought happens when it hasn't rained for a long time. We haven't had a good downpour in over two months! Things are starting to look real bad.

Sy Clone: In what way?

Farmer Famine: Just take a look around! My cornstalks are withering and the potatoes are drying up. I'm even finding it hard to keep the grass watered so the cows can graze.

Sy Clone: Gosh! You've got quite a problem!

Farmer Famine: Correction! *We*'ve got quite a problem. If I can't grow food, you don't eat!

Disaster News Network (DNN)
(A Radio Play cont.)

Sy Clone: You're right! This is *our* problem. What can we do about it?

Farmer Famine: Everyone can help by saving water. Don't waste it! We need all the water we can get.

Sy Clone: Thanks, Farmer Famine. Back to you Ava.

Ava Lanche: We'll have more news after this commercial break.

Commercial Announcer: You've asked for it and here it is! The record you've been waiting for! All your favorite hits from the 50s, 60s, and 70s! Listen to such classics as "All Shook Up" by the Quakes, "Up Up, and Away" by His and the Herricanes, and "It Never Rains In California" by Del and the Droughts. Order today and receive a bonus record, "Whole Lotta Shakin' Goin' On" by the Volcanoes. Only $15.99. Available on cassette or CD. Order today!

Ava Lanche: Welcome back. Now here's Hal Storm with today's weather report. Any rain in sight?

Hal Storm: I've got good news and bad news. There *is* a report of rain in sight, but it's in the form of a hurricane watch! That means a hurricane may be approaching our area. The weather radar shows that a lot of moisture in the air is collecting over the ocean. Once that moisture starts to rise and spiral—look out! And remember, hurricanes bring tornadoes with them, so if you see any funnel-shaped clouds, take cover! Ava?

Ava Lanche: Right you are, Hal! Hurricanes and tornadoes can be very dangerous. Now, time for sports. Our sports reporter, Rock Slyde, is on location at the World Series, many miles away. Who's winning, Rock?

(Sound effect: rain and thunder.)

Rock Slyde: The rain is, Ava. You may be having a drought, but here at the World Series, we could sure use a few rainless days! The last game between the Texas Twisters and the Florida Cyclones has been rained out again. The series is tied three to three but the rainy weather has postponed the tie-breaker game for two weeks. I'm here at Mudslide Stadium and the ball field is under three feet of water because of floods. Floods have damaged many of the roads and buildings here. Let's hope things dry up soon!

Ava Lanche: Thanks, Rock! In other news, our Travel Correspondent, Sue Nami, has been visiting tropical islands for our South Pacific Feature. Let's go there by remote satellite. Sue, are you there?

(Sound effect: tropical music.)

Sue Nami: Yes, Ava. I'm here on the beautiful island of Lava-Lava.

Ava Lanche: Lava-Lava? That's an unusual name for an island. What does it mean?

Sue Nami: I'm glad you asked that, Ava. Lava is hot, liquid rock that comes out of a volcano. Lava-Lava is an island made out of lava that erupted from an undersea volcano.

Ava Lanche: How can that be?

Sue Nami: Well, a volcano is a hole or crack in the surface of the Earth. Some of these holes are on land, but some are also on the ocean floor. There's hot, liquid rock called *magma* under the surface of the Earth. Magma can push up through a crack and come out on the Earth's surface as lava. When enough lava cools and piles up, it can form an island or a mountain! After a while, plants begin to grow on it and animals make their homes there.

Ava Lanche: Aren't you frightened to stay on an island made by a volcano?

Sue Nami: Well, an erupting volcano can be dangerous. Hot lava can quickly cover land and villages. But this island is a dormant, or sleeping, volcano. Scientists can check volcanos and warn people if they think it is going to erupt soon.

Ava Lanche: How interesting, Sue! I can hardly wait to see where you'll take us tomorrow!

Sue Nami: Good-bye till then, Ava!

Ava Lanche: Well, that's the news for tonight. Thanks for being with us and have a good evening. *The tape recorder is turned off.*

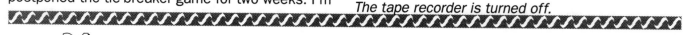

Regions of the World

Objective:
Students will be able to identify and distinguish between major physical regions of the world.

Background

The world in which we live is richly diverse. Some parts of the Earth are covered with hot, dry desert while other parts are cold and mountainous. Major regions of the world include:

1. **Grasslands,** also called *pampas, prairies,* or *steppes,* consist of flat or gently rolling countryside with a temperate, windy climate. Occasional rain brings grasses and flowers but not many trees to this area. The soil is suitable for many types of crops. North American grasslands support grazing and burrowing animals, such as bison and prairie dogs. Zebras, lions, and gazelles can be found on African plains, and cattle roam the South American pampas.

2. **Rain forests** are hot and wet. The trees grow so thick that little sunlight reaches the ground, leaving the soil unsuitable for many types of plants, except vines and ferns. Wildlife includes exotic birds, monkeys, and reptiles.

3. **Forests** or *woodlands* are found in temperate climates where the rich, organic soil is suitable for many trees, shrubs, flowers, and ground cover. Deer, rabbits, squirrels, and bears are some forest inhabitants.

4. **Mountains** are often windy, cold, and snow-capped. Since the rocky ground has little soil, vegetation is limited to low-lying ground cover and conifers. Mountain goats and birds of prey are some of the animals adapted to a mountainous environment.

5. **Deserts** are hot, dry, and often windy. Because of scarce rainfall and a rocky, sandy terrain there are usually few plants, the most common being cactus and other succulents. Lizards, camels, and snakes are some animals that inhabit deserts.

6. **Tundra**, in the polar regions, consists of cold and snowy stretches of barren land, supporting little vegetation. Wildlife includes reindeer, seals, and elk.

Materials

1. Reference materials.
2. Scissors.
3. A brad fastener.
4. Three pieces of 18 x 24-inch white tagboard.
5. A black marker.
6. A razor blade or sharp-pointed knife.
7. A shoebox.
8. Half-a-dozen sheets of different writing paper.

For each group:

9. A copy of the Regions Study Sheet (page 38).

Preparation

Construct the following "Dial-a-Region" wheel ahead of time:

a. On the tagboard, trace and cut out four circles with these approximate diameters: 17 1/2, 15, 12, and 9 inches.

b. Divide the largest circle into six equal parts using the black marker.

c. On the outside edge of the largest circle, label the sections: Desert, Mountain, Tundra, Forest, Rain Forest, Grassland.

d. Using a sharp-edged blade, carefully cut windows into all but the largest circle, as illustrated below.

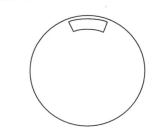

e. Beside each window write a label: WILD LIFE on the second-largest circle, PLANT LIFE & SOIL on the third-largest, and CLIMATE on the smallest.

f. Stack the circles in order from the largest at the bottom to the smallest on top. Center them and then attach them all together with a brad fastener in the middle. The finished wheel should look like this:

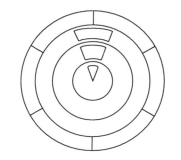

Write the word "Mail" on the sides of the shoe box. Write the following letters on different pieces of writing paper.

1. Dear Boys and Girls,

How are you? My name is Leandro and I live on a high mountain in the Andes of Peru, which is in South America. My family raises llamas. Llamas have soft, warm fur that we make into sweaters and coats. I am glad to have such clothing, because it gets very cold here!
Your friend,
Leandro

2. Dear Students,

Greetings from the land of ice and snow! We had three inches of snow last night. Today, my father took us for a long dog sled ride over some frozen water. You can go most any place with a sled and dog team. Do you have much snow? We have lots of snow and ice. Watch out for polar bears!
Kirima

3. Dear Class,

My name is Emily and I am a member of the Sioux Indian tribe. My Native American name is Chumani. That means "dewdrops" in my native language. Long ago, my ancestors hunted buffalo that ate the sweet grasses around my home. Today, the buffalo are gone but the grass is still here, along with many pretty flowers. It is winter now. My parents have a farm. Everyone helps out. It is my job to feed our chickens. Will you write me back?
Emily

4. Greetings, Friends!

I am Ajani and I live in a small village in the Congo Republic. Today it was very hot, and I spent much time in the shady rain forest helping collect cocoa pods. Cocoa is used in making chocolate, and we cut the pods from trees. Sometimes I put the pods in a bag. There were lots of monkeys in the trees today, watching us work. They sure make a lot of noise!
Your friend,
Ajani

5. Hello!

My name is Rafi and I tend goats. Water and grass are hard to find where I live in the desert, so my family and I live in a tent. We carry the tent with us as we search for places where our goats can eat and drink. Sometimes the wind here blows so hard I can feel the sand right through my clothing. What is it like where you live?
Rafi

6. Dear Students,

I am from the country of Germany. My name is Marta and I go to school, too. When I come home from school I like to take a walk in the woods behind my house, if it's not too rainy or cold. I pretend many things. Sometimes I sit under a tree and tell the squirrels stories. Where do you like to play?
Goodbye for now,
Marta

Place the letters in the shoebox.

Activity

To build interest, begin by showing students the "mailbox" and telling them that the class has received some letters from imaginary pen pals. Invite several students to read letters aloud. Discuss how the letters are similar and dissimilar to one another with leading questions such as "What type of weather does each pen pal have?" and "What kinds of animals does Ajani see? Does he see the same kind of animals that Rafi sees?" Bring up and define words like climate, soil, plant life, and wildlife.

Next, tell the students that each pen pal lives in a different region, or part, of the world, and that today they are going to find out more about these regions. Distribute the Regions Study Sheet and assign each group one of the six regions to research.

After allowing time for groups to complete the chart, have each group spokesperson report on the gathered information. Use this information to complete the Dial-a-Region wheel together as a class. For example, when the Desert Region spokesperson reports, move all three windows so they align under the Desert section of the wheel. Beginning with Wildlife, fill in each section as you go along. Keep the completed Dial-a-Region posted for future reference.

Extension

Reread the letters from the pen pals and have the students decide which region each writer lives in. Ask them to tell what clues about the region were in each letter. Next, let the students write to one of the fictional pen pals, describing the region they live in.

Regions Study Sheet

Our region is _____ .
Find out as much as you can about each topic, filling in that part of the circle.
Remember to work together and be ready to share your research with the rest of the class.

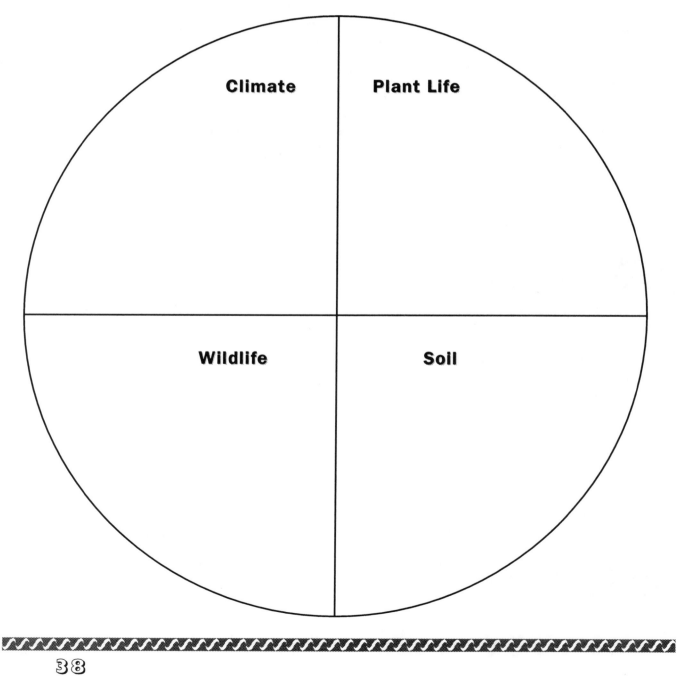

The Ocean

Objective:
Students will be able to identify the Earth's oceans and describe their major resources.

Background

Water covers three-fourths of the Earth's surface. This large body of water can be divided into four oceans—the Pacific, Atlantic, Indian, and Arctic—of which the Pacific Ocean is the largest and deepest and the Arctic is the smallest and shallowest. Ocean water contains many dissolved minerals, including salt, gold, and silver. The minerals are washed into streams and rivers and carried out into the ocean.

The ocean is in a constant state of movement. Waves, caused by wind blowing across the water surface, can range in height from less than one inch (ripples) to over 100 feet, depending on how hard and long the wind blows. Ocean currents are warm or cold horizontal movements of water also caused by the wind. Tides are the regular rising and falling of ocean waters caused by the shifting pull of gravity as the moon revolves around the Earth.

The ocean has an abundance of plant and animal life which supports a large and active fishing industry.

Materials

1. Reference materials.

2. One sheet each of red, white, and blue construction paper.
3. A black marker.
4. A hole punch (or one for each group if possible).

For each group:
5. Colored markers or crayons.
6. 1-inch diameter loose leaf rings (available at office supply stores; or loops of string may be used instead).
7. A large box (such as grocery box).
8. Construction paper scraps.
9. Glue.
10. Scissors.
11. String.
12. Adhesive tape.
13. Blue and brown poster paint (sandpaper may be used instead of brown paint: see Extension).
14. Brushes.
15. (optional) Shells and coral.

For each student:
16. A set of Ocean Facts Flash Cards

Preparation

Begin ahead of time to collect enough cardboard boxes for each small group. Remove the top flaps.

Activity

Begin the lesson by folding a white piece of construction paper in half (diagonally) and cutting one of the triangles, as illustrated.

Tape this piece to the chalkboard (this is the sail of a boat). Next, take a red piece of paper and, holding it lengthwise, cut as illustrated:

Tape this piece (the boat hull) below the sail. Now take a small piece of blue paper, cut it into a small triangle, as illustrated, and tape it to the top of the sail.

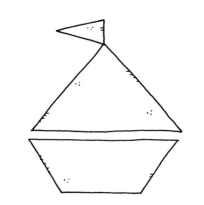

Talk with the class about places where they might see a sailboat. When someone suggests the ocean, tell the students that that is where this sailboat will be going. Write the words "Ocean Resources" on the red hull of the boat. Explain to the students that resources are things that we can use or enjoy. Brainstorm with the class a list of things that we can use or enjoy from the ocean. Write this list on the sail part of the sailboat.

Next, distribute the Ocean Facts Flash Cards and ask the students to cut them apart. Have them read the cards and research the answers with other group members. They should write the answers on the back of each card. The students may then color and hole-punch the cards

and attach them to a ring binder (or thread string through the holes and tie the ends). When the flash card set is complete, have the students take turns "flashing" facts to each other and checking their answers.

Answers to Ocean Facts:
1. 71 percent
2. oil
3. wind
4. salt
5. gravity
6. seafood
7. oysters
8. Pacific
9. Pacific, Atlantic, Indian, and Arctic

Extension

Provide each group with a large box, scrap construction paper, glue, scissors, string, tape, poster paints, and brushes, and have each group design an ocean diorama. Have the students paint the bottom inside of the box brown (or cover it with sandpaper) and the other sides blue. Using reference books, they should draw, color, and label the different resources the ocean has to offer. They can glue pictures to the background or "ocean floor" or suspend them with string taped to the top of the box sides. They might add pieces of shell or coral for a realistic touch. When the dioramas are finished, tape plastic wrap over the "viewing section" and display them in the classroom.

Ocean Facts
Flash Cards

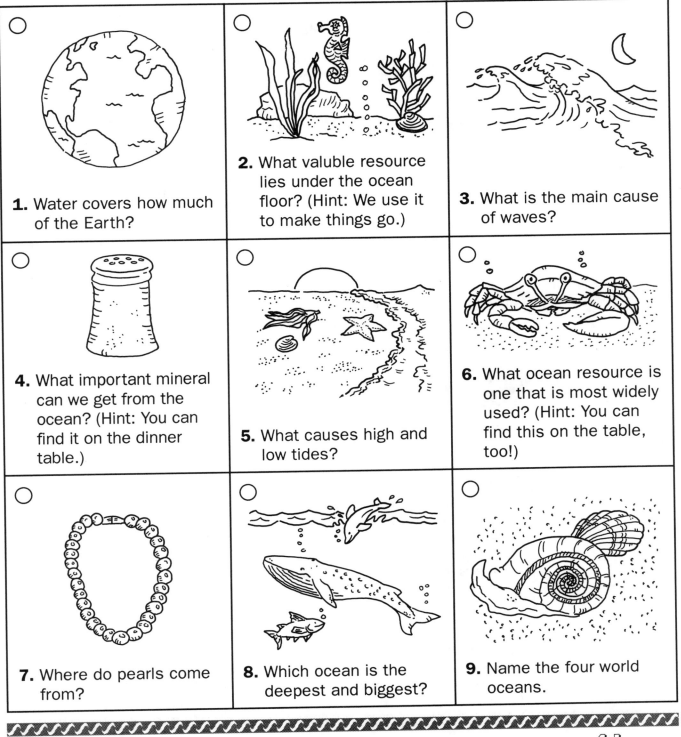

1. Water covers how much of the Earth?

2. What valuble resource lies under the ocean floor? (Hint: We use it to make things go.)

3. What is the main cause of waves?

4. What important mineral can we get from the ocean? (Hint: You can find it on the dinner table.)

5. What causes high and low tides?

6. What ocean resource is one that is most widely used? (Hint: You can find this on the table, too!)

7. Where do pearls come from?

8. Which ocean is the deepest and biggest?

9. Name the four world oceans.

Natural Resources

Objective:
Students will distinguish between natural resources and manufactured products.

Background

As stated earlier, a resource is something that can be used or enjoyed. Natural resources are usable things that nature provides, such as water, land, and their products. Soil, water, and air are basic resources necessary for our survival, while other resources, such as woodlands and wildlife, are important in maintaining an ecological balance. In addition, people use all kinds of natural resources to manufacture objects or other resources.

Materials

1. A variety of magazines.
2. String.
3. A hole punch.

For each group:

4. An assortment of natural materials (rocks, fruit, wood chips, metal, shells, etc.).
5. An assortment of manufactured objects (jewelry, small knickknacks, glove, etc.).
6. A shoebox.

For each student:

7. A wire hanger (see Preparation).
8. Scissors.
9. Construction paper scraps.
10. Glue.

Preparation

In advance, ask each student to bring in a wire hanger.

Cut a 2 1/2-inch diameter circle in the middle of each shoebox lid. Fill each box with a variety of natural and manufactured materials (avoid any with sharp edges) and tape the box closed.

Activity

Make two columns on the chalkboard. Label one column YES and the other NO. Say the word "gold" and pause a moment; then say "yes" and write "gold" under the YES column. Next say the word "jewelry," pause, say "no," and write "jewelry" under the NO column. Continue with words such as the following:

wood—YES
furniture—NO
water—YES
soda—NO
animal—YES
fur coat—NO

After a while stop and ask if anyone understands the pattern. Then ask for more items to add to each list. Help the students to see that each "yes" word is something found in nature, unchanged by people. Point out that all of the "no" words have parts taken from nature but have been changed in some way by people. Explain that the "yes" words are called *natural resources*—useful things produced by nature.

Next, distribute a shoebox to each group. Tell the class that each box is filled with natural and manufactured resources. The students are going to take turns guessing which resources are in the box. Each member will insert a hand in the opening, pick up an object, and without removing it from the box attempt to describe it by using the sense of touch. After guessing what the object is, the student can pull it from the box to see if the guess was correct. Students should hold onto their object until every group member has had a turn. When the guessing is completed, have each student stand up, show the object, and tell whether it is natural or manufactured. If it is manufactured, have students identify what part of the object was originally a natural resource.

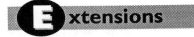

Extensions

- Invite the students to make a resource mobile. Using magazines, have the students find at least five pictures of natural resources. Students should cut out the pictures and glue them to small pieces of construction paper. Then, they should punch holes (near the top), thread string through the holes, and tie the ends to the wire hanger. Hang the completed mobiles in the room.

- Use the Feature Presentation Bulletin Board on page 88 to round out this activity.

Human Resources

Objective:
Students will be able to discuss the variety of resources that people can provide with different kinds of skills and labor.

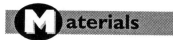ackground

People also are resources. Just as natural resources make our lives better, so do the skills and services that people offer. This contribution can be classified into two groups: *goods* and *services*. The farmer who grows vegetables to sell is offering a good. The doctor who sets a broken arm is providing a service. Goods are tangible products, while services are acts of assistance.

aterials

1. A variety of magazines.

For each group:

2. A small box.
3. A set of Occupation Game Cards (page 45).
4. Glue.
5. String.
6. Scissors.
7. Construction paper scraps.

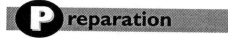reparation

Reproduce a set of Occupation Game Cards for each small group. Cut the cards apart and place a set in each box.

ctivity

Conduct an informal class survey by asking students to name different jobs. List each job on the chalkboard. Remind students of the definition of a resource—something usable—and go over the list again, discussing the contribution each job makes. Explain to the students that people are resources, too, and that they use their jobs to either make or sell a good (product) or perform a service. Classify the chalkboard list into GOODS and SERVICES.

Give each group a box containing the Occupation Game Cards. Direct students to take turns picking a card and silently reading the occupation, which they now pretend is theirs. Other group members will try to guess the job by asking questions that can be answered only by "yes," "no," or "I don't know." Each student may ask three questions (one at a time), after which a guess may be made (a guess counts as a question). Play continues until all members have had two turns choosing cards. (Encourage students to ask good- or service-oriented questions such as "Do you make something?" or "Do you help people?")

xtensions

- Have the students look through the supply of magazines to find pictures of people using a skill. They should then attach at least two pictures to the mobile from the previous lesson (see page 43).
- Use the Hats Off! (page 90) or What's in a Name (page 98) Bulletin Boards to round out this activity.

Occupation Game Cards

Doctor	Carpenter	Counselor
Cook	Gardener	Pilot
Ballet Dancer	Artist	Teacher
Construction Worker	Soldier	Seamstress or Tailor

Using Resources

Objective:
Students will explore some of the ways in which people use natural resources.

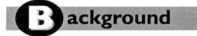

Background

From the earliest times, people have used materials and the skills they possess to make life better. Before the days of worldwide trade, people mainly used the resources available in their region, and these greatly influenced the development of each regional community. People who settled in forest areas built homes made of wood and developed lumber and fur trades. People living near the ocean built homes of stone or brick and went into the fishing trade. Later, as more trade routes developed and transportation became more sophisticated, people had more choice in the types of resources they used.

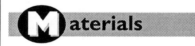

Materials

1. Reference materials.

For each group:

2. A set of Situation Cards (page 48).
3. A Profile Sheet (page 49).
4. Two or three scissors.
5. Adhesive tape.
6. Several sheets of plain paper.
7. A box of crayons.

For each student:

8. A copy of the Story Frame Booklet (page 50).

Preparation

This activity works best with a group of four or fewer members. After you have copied the Situation Cards, cut them apart.

Activity

Go to each group and distribute the group materials. Provide one group member with the sheets of paper, give the scissors to another, the roll of tape to another, and so on, until all the group materials have been distributed. Assign each student to try to build a tabletop house in one minute using only the items given to him or her. At the end of the minute, ask students to describe any difficulties they had completing the assignment. Of course, they will have had considerable difficulty, especially those with nothing but scissors. Ask students to suggest what would make the task easier. Elicit the response that being able to use all of the materials possessed by the group members would make the task easier.

Next, tell the students they will have a second chance to build a house, but this time they can work together as a group and share all the materials. Allow them several minutes to work, and observe them working together. At the end, have students compare their first house with the second house they built together. Help the students to see how working together and using a variety of materials made the job easier and resulted in a better house. Point out to the class that today people can work together and

share their resources, but it was not always this way.

Long ago, people lived farther apart and had no easy means of contact with one another. They therefore had less choice in the types of resources they could use. Ask the students to imagine that they are settlers going to live in an area uninhabited by others. How will they start out their new life? Where will they live? What will they eat? How will they dress?

Tell the class that you are going to give each group a Situation Card that describes a particular place. Using reference materials, they should fill in a Profile Sheet, remembering that they will be the first human inhabitants of that area, and should take into account climate, plant life, and wildlife conditions in planning their new life. At the end of the research time, allow the group spokespersons to share their Profile Sheets with the rest of the class.

Extension

Have students assemble the Story Frame Booklet as follows:

a. Cut along solid lines. (Students should each have three rectangles.)
b. Fold each page section where indicated.
c. Glue the back of page 1 to the back of the cover.
d. Glue the back of page 2 to the back of page 3.
e. Glue the back of page 4 to the inside back cover.

Have each student fill in the spaces, using the information contained in their group Profile Sheets. Allow students to share their books with one another.

Situation Cards

The woodlands of Maine	The Atlantic coast of Maryland
A desert in old-time Arizona	The tundra of what is now Alaska
A mountain in what is now Kentucky	The grasslands of what is now called Kansas

Profile Sheet

You and a small group of others have left your old country to make a home in a new land. You have brought very little with you, and must start from almost nothing. Fill in this Profile Sheet to help you get started.

Use reference books to help your group answer these questions about your new home.

1. What is your climate like?

_____

2. a. What type of soil do you have?

_____

b. What can you plant in this type of soil?

_____

3. What other types of plants or trees are there?

_____

4. What kinds of wildlife will you see around your new home?

_____

5. What land and water features are there?

_____

These things are your *natural resources*. You must use these resources as well as your own skills to survive. As a group, decide on answers to the following questions:

6. What type of shelter will you build? (You have a few tools you brought with you from the old country.) _____

7. What kind of clothes will you wear and what will you make them out of? (Remember the weather!) _____

8. What types of food will you eat?_____

9. There are some traders who come through your area now and then. What will you offer to trade? _____

10. What will you want in return? _____

Story Frame Booklet

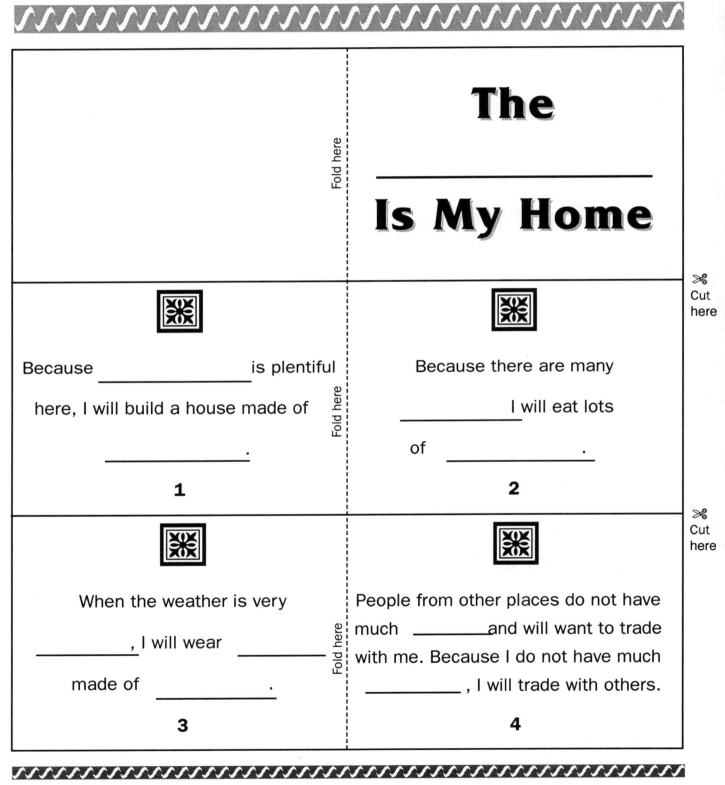

The

_____

Is My Home

✂ Cut here

Because _____ is plentiful

here, I will build a house made of

_____ .

1

Because there are many

_____ I will eat lots

of _____ .

2

✂ Cut here

When the weather is very

_____ , I will wear _____

made of _____ .

3

People from other places do not have

much _____ and will want to trade

with me. Because I do not have much

_____ , I will trade with others.

4

Using a Globe

Objective:
Students will explore the main features of a globe.

Background

A globe is a miniature model of the Earth. Unlike maps, which are flat, a globe can give a better idea of how land and water features look. Like maps, most globes have imaginary lines drawn on them to help us locate specific areas. These lines, measured in degrees, are called latitude and longitude. Lines of latitude start at the widest part of the Earth and divide it into the Northern and Southern Hemispheres. Lines of longitude pass through the North and South Poles and divide the Earth into the Eastern and Western Hemispheres. Other lines of interest on a globe include the Equator (where lines of latitude start at 0°) and the Prime Meridian (where lines of longitude start at 0°).

Materials

1. A globe (the largest available).
2. Newspapers (see Preparation).
3. Papier mâché (see Preparation).

For each group:

4. A large bowl.
5. Green, blue, and brown poster paints.

For each student:

6. A round balloon.
7. String.
8. A paintbrush.

9. A black marker.

Preparation

Collect newspapers ahead of time. You will need enough to cover all desks and to provide strips for papier mâché.

To make papier mâché you will need either a premixed powder or one of the following sets of ingredients (available in a hardware store or large chain store):

• 9 cups of wallpaper paste mix plus 11 cups of water, or
• 8 cups of plaster of paris plus 2 teaspoons of commercial white glue.

Background

Present the class with the globe and have them tell you what they know about a globe. Review the names of the four oceans and locate them on the globe. Point out the large masses of land and introduce the idea of *continents* to the students. Write the names of the seven continents on the board and locate them on the globe. Direct the students' attention to the different types of lines drawn on the globe and briefly discuss their functions.

Tell the class that a globe is a map of the Earth that is also shaped like the Earth, and that today they will be making their own globes. Distribute a balloon and piece of string to each student. Have the students blow up their balloons and tie them securely.

Instruct the students to begin tearing newspaper into long strips. Then mix the papier mâché for each group's bowl.

(With premixed powder, follow the directions on the box. With either of the two recipes, place the ingredients in the bowl and mix well.) Students should dip the strips into the bowl, squeeze off the excess with their fingers, and carefully wrap each strip around the balloon until all surfaces are covered, taking care to retain the round shape. Hang the "globes" up to dry.

When the globes are dry, have the students paint land masses and bodies of water, using the regular globe as a model. When the paint is dry, students can use a black marker to label the continents, oceans, North and South Poles, Equator, and Prime Meridian.

Extension

Using balloons blown to various sizes, have the groups make the other planets in our Solar System, along with the Sun and Moon. Cover each with papier mâché, paint with appropriate colors, and hang them from the ceiling (in order, beginning with the Sun).

Exploring Cultures

Objective:
Students will explore and appreciate different ways of life around the world.

Background

Many different groups of people make up our world, and each group has its own special customs and manners that make up its culture. People are similar in many ways: We have arms, legs, heads, and hair; we eat, talk, and sleep; and we all learn, work, and play. The differences between peoples revolve around the way we do various things, the way we think about things, and the way we live. These are called customs.

Materials

1. A globe or a wall map of the world.
2. Reference materials.
3. A piece of chart paper (optional).
4. Fifteen strips of fairly heavy white paper, each 6 x 2 inches.
5. String.

For each group:

6. A copy of the Cultural Study Sheet (page 55).
7. A rectangular sheet of white construction paper.
8. Scraps of colored construction paper.
9. Markers and/or crayons.
10. Scissors.
11. Glue.

Preparation

On each copy of the Cultural Study Sheet, write one of the following country names in the top line: China, Italy, Australia, Zaire, Canada, Argentina. Copy the chart below on the blackboard or on a piece of chart paper.

On each of the 15 strips of paper, write one set of the following words, leaving about 2 inches of space after the

Cultures of the World									
Country	Location	Population	Trans-portation	Crops	Goods	Food	Architec-ture	Language	Govern-ment
China									
Italy									
Australia									
Zaire									
Canada									
Argentina									

place name. (Do not include the pronunciations.)

France—Bonjour [bawn-ZHOOR]

Mexico—Buenos días [BWEH-nos DEE-ahs]

Japan—Konnichi wa [kon-nee-chee WAH]

Hawaii—Aloha [ah-LOH-hah]

Germany—Guten Tag [GOO-tun TAHG]

Greece—Geia [GIGH-uh]

Norway—Hallo [HAH-lo]

Italy—Ciao [chow]

Brazil—Aló [ah-LOH]

Russia—Zdrasdvuite [z'DRASS-vooy-teh, or simply z'DRASS-teh]

Iran—Salam [sah-LAHM]

Nigeria—Pele [PEL-eh]

Turkey—Gunaydin [goo-nigh-DIN]

Poland—Dzien dobry [JEN DOB-ree]

China—Ni hao [NEE how].

Carefully cut each sentence strip in half with a distinct wavy or zigzag line, different for each strip. You should now have 30 strips, with the name of a country or place on half of the pieces and a greeting on the remaining half.

Activity

Distribute the sentence strips to all class members. Explain that half of the students have the names of places on their strips, while the other half have strips with greetings in the languages of these places. Ask each "place" student to find the "greeting" student that has the piece that fits his or her strip. When all the matches have been made, have each pair tape their strips together on the board. Assist the students with pronouncing the greetings and locating their "home" on a wall map or globe.

Discuss other differences that these countries or places have from one another, such as food or dress. Tell the class they will take time today to explore

these differences at a deeper level. Distribute the Cultural Study Sheet to each group and assign a country—China, Italy, Australia, Argentina, Canada, or Zaire. Have students use the reference materials to answer each question.

Later, complete the prepared chart by asking the group spokespersons to share their information. Discuss the contents of the chart and ways in which people are alike and different. Stress the fact that everyone can make a valuable contribution to our world.

Extensions

- Distribute a piece of white construction paper to each group. Have the students draw a line down the left side of the paper, about one inch from the edge. Leaving this margin blank, they should use markers, crayons, and scrap paper to create a flag of their assigned country. Then, they should glue the study sheet to the back of the completed flag and fold each flag along the drawn line. Take a long piece of string to each group in turn. Each group should place the string into the fold of its flag and glue the flap down. The finished product will be a line of flags that you can hang in the classroom.

- Use the Games Around the World Bulletin Board on page 103 to round out this activity.

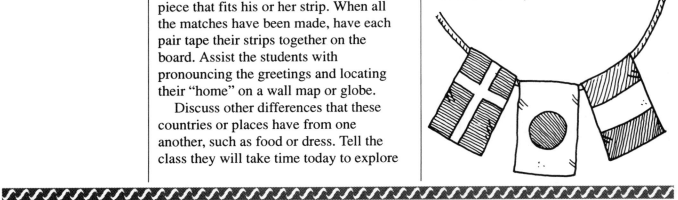

Cultural Study Sheet

Our country is _____.

1. Our country is located on the continent of _____.

2. There are _____ people living here.

3. People use _____ to get around.

4. They grow _____ here.

5. They make _____ here.

6. They like to eat _____.

7. People here live in _____ made of _____.

8. _____ is the language most of the people speak.

9. They have a _____ type of government. That means

that _____.

10. _____ and _____

are some interesting things to see here.

Objective:
Students will explore the major elements of maps.

Background

Maps can do more than just indicate the location of places. Maps can show direction, distance, land and water features, altitudes, and items of interest. To use a map easily, however, it helps to be familiar with the parts of a map:

1. Symbols represent landmarks and waterways.
2. Borderlines indicate where one section of land ends and another begins.
3. The scale of miles measures distances.
4. The compass rose points out cardinal (north, west, south, and east) and ordinal (northwest, southeast, etc.) directions.

Materials

1. A globe.
2. A large-scale map of your community showing your school.

Station 1:
3. Various maps with easy-to-read symbols.
4. Four sets of Symbol Match Cards (enough for each pair in a group).
5. Index cards (enough for each student).
6. Crayons.

Station 2:
7. Copies of the Connect-a-Dot map (see Preparation).

8. A map of your state (with neighboring states shown).
9. Yarn.
10. Glue.
11. Scissors.

Station 3:
12. Copies of the Vacationland map (page 62).
13. Colored markers.
14. Scraps of paper.
15. Pencils.
16. Rulers.

Station 4:
17. A small clear dish or bowl filled with water.
18. A needle.
19. The upper, wider half of a cork.
20. A bar magnet.
21. A copy of the Compass Rose (page 63).

For each student:
22. A copy of the Looking at Maps worksheets (pages 58–60).

Preparation

Divide the class into four groups and follow the same rotation process as in Natural Changers (page 25).

In advance, collect a variety of maps, including the state map and large-scale community map. Make an outline of your state using dots and numbers, as in this example:

TENNESSEE

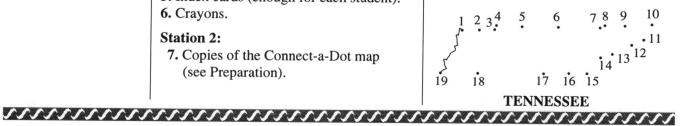

Make the appropriate number of copies of this outline, the Looking at Maps worksheets (pages 58–60), the Symbol Match Cards (page 61), the Vacationland map (page 62), and the Compass Rose (page 63).

Draw a scaled-down seating chart on the board, using index card-sized spaces for the students' desks. Clearly indicate classroom landmarks, such as the teacher's desk and bookcases. Keep some tape nearby.

Prepare each station with the listed materials and label as follows:

Station 1: Symbols

Station 2: Boundaries

Station 3: Scale of Miles

Station 4: Compass Rose

 **Activity**

Ask the students to imagine that they are once again aliens flying over the Earth in a spaceship. Tell them it is time to visit a typical Earthling school, and the one selected is yours. Using a globe, ask if it is possible to locate the school when viewing the entire Earth. Help students to see the difficulty of pinpointing such a tiny spot on the globe. Discuss other ways that the outer space visitor could find the school. When the suggestion "map" comes up, display the map of your town that shows the location of your school.

Indicate to the students that although this map shows the school, there are certain things we need to know about the map before it can really help us. Write the words symbol, boundary, scale of miles, and compass rose on the board. Tell the students that today they will be visiting four stations that will help them learn more about these items, and why they are such important tools in understanding maps.

Review with students the procedure for rotating to each station and how they should use their time at each station:

Station 1. Each pair will first play the Symbol Match Game. Then students will design a symbol representing themselves and tape it to the correct place on the chalkboard seating chart.

Station 2. Students will connect the dots on the outline to reveal their state, and then carefully glue a yarn "border" around its edges. Using the state map as a guide, they will identify and label neighboring states.

Station 3. Each student will select a different color marker and trace a different path from "Home" to a favorite Vacationland location. When everyone has had a turn, each student adds up his or her miles to see who wins the race. (The student with the smallest number of miles wins.)

Station 4. At this station, students will construct a compass and use it to sketch a mini-map of the classroom. (Note: Constructing the compass involves pushing the needle through the cork, and cleanup involves removing the needle. For safety, you may wish to tell students that you will handle these procedures.)

Distribute a copy of the Looking at Maps worksheet to each student. Divide the class into groups and arrange partners for Station 1. At the signal, have groups move from station to station. Give them a five-minute warning signal for cleanup.

 **Extension**

Use the Land of Make-Believe (page 94) or How's the Weather (page 101) Bulletin Boards to round out this activity.

Looking at Maps

Maps are full of interesting information! Visit each of the stations below and find out about four different "tools" used on maps to help us learn.

Station 1: Symbols

Symbols are pictures that stand for something else. On a map, symbols show places that are too big to draw clearly on a map.

Look at the maps on the table. Each map has a special part called a *legend* or *key*. It is usually in a corner. A legend shows you what each symbol on the map stands for. What symbols do you see?

Now, with a partner, take a set of Symbol Match Cards. Half of the cards show symbols; the other half describe them. Take turns matching symbols and descriptions with your partner.

When you are through, take an index card and draw a symbol that stands for you. For example, if you like to read, your symbol could be a book. Take your finished picture to the class seating chart on the chalkboard. Tape your symbol to your "seat."

Cleanup: Restack the Symbol Match cards.

Station 2: Boundaries

A *boundary*, or *border*, is an imaginary line that separates one place from another. On a map, it is drawn as a real line. Boundaries help people to know where their land ends and where someone else's land begins.

Look at the Connect-a-Dot picture. What do you think it is a picture of? Connect the dots to find out!

When you are finished you should have an outline of our state. Write the name of our state in the middle of the outline. Look at the map of our state on the table. What states surround our state? Write their names on the Connect-a-Dot map where they belong.

Now make a boundary line for our state to help show where our state ends and another state or area begins. Cut off a piece of yarn and carefully glue it around the outline. You've just made a boundary!

Cleanup: Write your name on the state outline and put it out of the way to dry. Make sure you have closed the glue bottles.

Looking at Maps (cont.)

Station 3: Scale of Miles

A *scale of miles* helps answer the question "How far?" Look at the Vacationland map and find the small line (it looks like a ruler) near the top. This is the scale of miles. It is usually one inch long, but it stands for a certain number of miles.

Look at the scale again. How many miles does it say 1 inch stands for? 10 miles is correct. Now, have each group member take a different colored marker. Starting at "Home", have each group member trace a path to a different vacation spot.

After everyone has traced a path, measure the distances and fill in the chart below. (Use a ruler to find how many inches it took to get from Home to each place. Since each inch is 10 miles long, you must multiply your total number of inches by 10. For example, if your route was 6 inches long, the distance traveled was 60 miles.)

	Name	Location	Inches	Mileage (Inches x 10)
1.				
2.				
3.				
4.				
5.				
6.				

Cleanup: Give your Vacationland map to your teacher.

Looking at Maps (cont.)

Station 4: Compass Rose

A *compass rose* is a drawing on a map that shows "which way"—directions such as north, south, east, and west. A compass rose can also show directions in between, like northeast and southwest. Compass roses are named for a tool called a *compass*. A compass shows directions in the real world. Follow these instructions to make your own compass:

1. Stroke a needle with the magnet. Move the end of the magnet along the needle about 30 or 40 times. Always stroke the needle in the same direction. Lift the magnet away from the needle when you move it back for each new stroke.
2. Carefully stick the needle through the sides of the piece of cork.
3. Place the cork in the dish of water. The needle should point north.

How does this happen? The Earth has an invisible force called *magnetism*. This magnetism is felt by pieces of iron (magnets are made from iron). If an iron needle is rubbed by a magnet, it becomes a magnet, too. It will then point north, toward the Earth's Magnetic North Pole.

Now slowly lift the dish up and slide the picture of the compass rose underneath. Line up the paper so that "North" is pointing in the same direction as the needle. Look at where the needle is pointing. What is in that direction in the room? What is in the south part of the room? Make a simple map of your classroom using the back of this page.

Cleanup: Remove the needle from the cork. Wipe up any spills. Remove the paper compass rose from under the dish.

Symbol Match Cards

Capital City	Wildlife Refuge	Airport	Hospital
City	Park	Railroad	College

Name _____

Vacationland

Vacationland

O | | |
1 inch = 10 miles
Scale of Miles

Ski
Mountain

Thriller
Amusement
Park

Fisherman's
Lake

Home

Wilderness Woods

Sightseeing City

Suntan Beach

Compass Rose

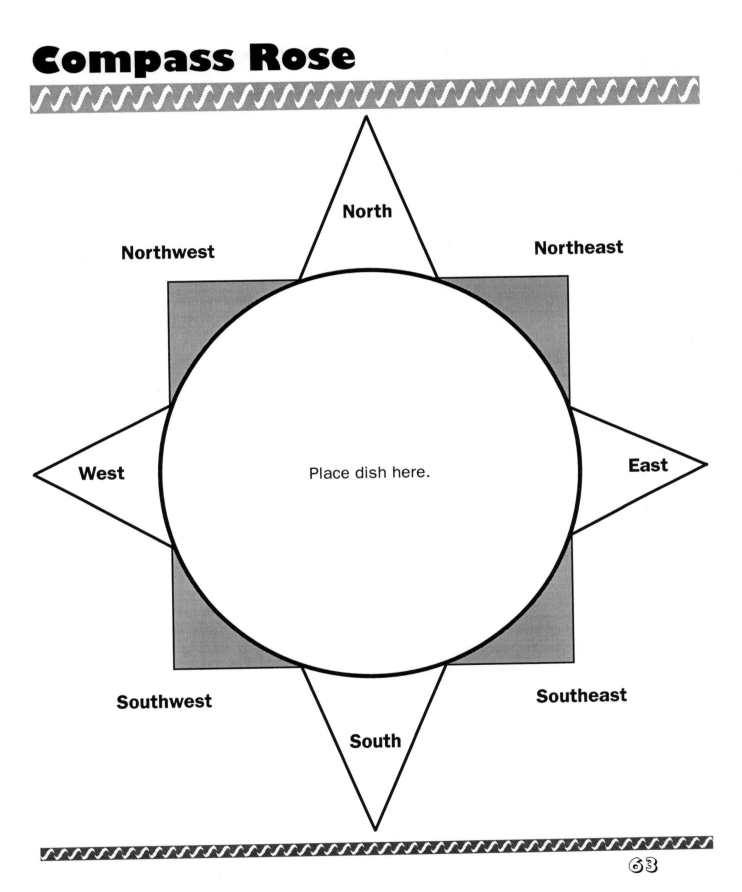

North

Northwest

Northeast

West

Place dish here.

East

Southwest

Southeast

South

Finding Places

Objective:
Students will locate positions on a map by using grid lines (coordinates).

Background

A grid is a pattern of intersecting lines that helps us find places on a map quickly and accurately. The lines running vertically are usually lettered in alphabetical order, while the horizontal lines are sequentially numbered. The lines are called *coordinates*. Places on a map can be identified and located by the letter and number of the nearest intersecting coordinates.

Materials

1. A large-scale map of your community.
2. Twenty-four 5 x 7-inch index cards.
3. A marker.
4. A sheet of chart paper.
5. Eight 5-foot lengths of string.
6. Adhesive or masking tape.
7. A marker.

For each group:

8. A copy of the Dinosaur Island map (page 66).
9. A copy of the Coordinate Slips (page 67).
10. A large open-mouthed plastic jar.

Preparation

Group 16 of the index cards into 8 pairs. Print a letter (A–D) or a number (1–4) on each pair. On the remaining 8 cards, print the name of a local town or landmark. Write an index (like the one shown below) on the chart paper, substituting the 8 names you wrote on the index cards for the blanks.

INDEX

A1 _____	B2 _____
C1 _____	D2 _____
A3 _____	B4 _____
C3 _____	D4 _____

For the extension, cut the coordinate slips apart and put a set into each group's jar.

Activity

Start the lesson by reminding students how difficult it was to locate the school using just a globe. Point out that it was easier to use a map, but students still needed help in locating the school. Discuss how difficult it would be to find an unknown place by just looking at a map. Tell the students that there is an easier and quicker way to find locations.

Invite the students to an open area in the room and direct them to sit in a circle. Distribute the index cards (having two students share each of the local town and landmark cards). Have the two students holding **A** cards take hold of opposite ends of a string and lay it on the floor. Secure each end with tape, and tape the **A** cards over the ends. Repeat the procedure with the **B**, **C**, and **D** cards. The strings should be placed parallel, about a foot apart. Repeat the procedure again with cards **1-4**, perpendicular to and crossing over the lettered strings. You should then have a grid similar to this:

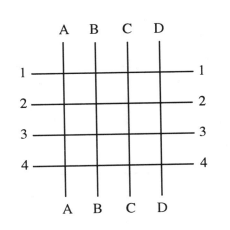

Point out how the two sets of lines cross and how each line has the same number or letter at either end. Explain that each line is called a *coordinate*, and the point where two coordinates cross can be given a name—their letter and number. To better illustrate, use your fingers to "walk" down the letter line and across the number line until they meet.

Ask those students holding cards with place names or landmarks to find their coordinates on the prepared Index. Using the coordinates from the Index, have the students "walk" their fingers along the correct letter and number lines until they meet. Once students have found the correct location, tape the index card to that spot. Repeat until all 8 cards have been placed.

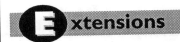

Extensions

- Ask students to rescue some shipwrecked sailors! Give each group a copy of the Dinosaur Island map and explain that survivors of a shipwreck are scattered over the island. Each castaway has written his or her coordinates on a piece of paper.

Group members take turns pulling a coordinate slip from the jar. They then locate the position and mark it on the map with an X. Repeat until all the castaways have been "rescued."

- Use the All-Star Game Bulletin Board on page 92 to round out this activity.

Dinosaur Island

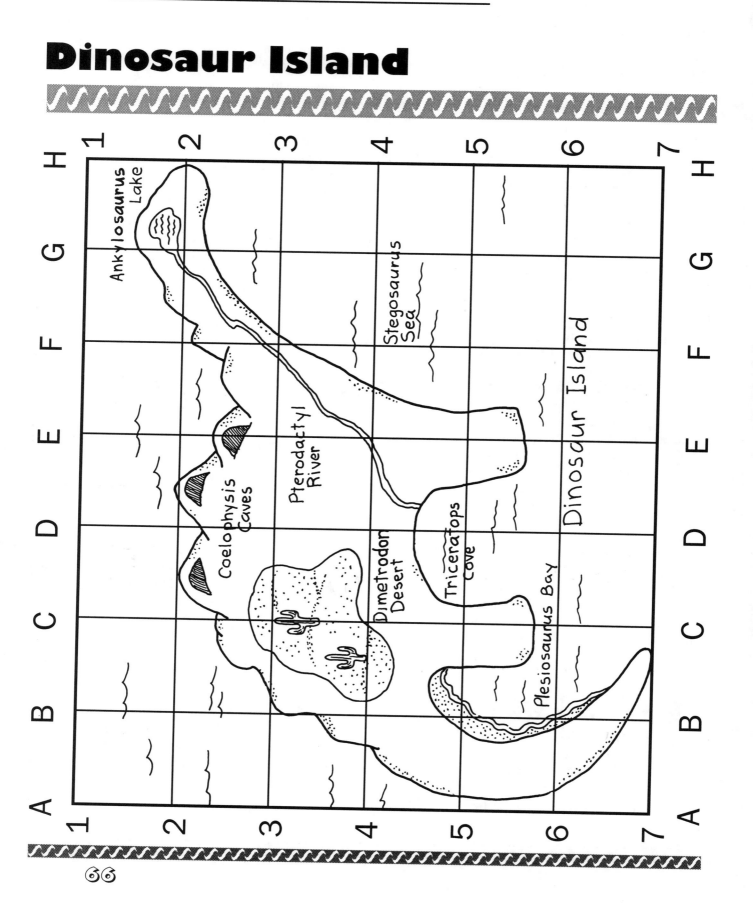

Coordinate Slips

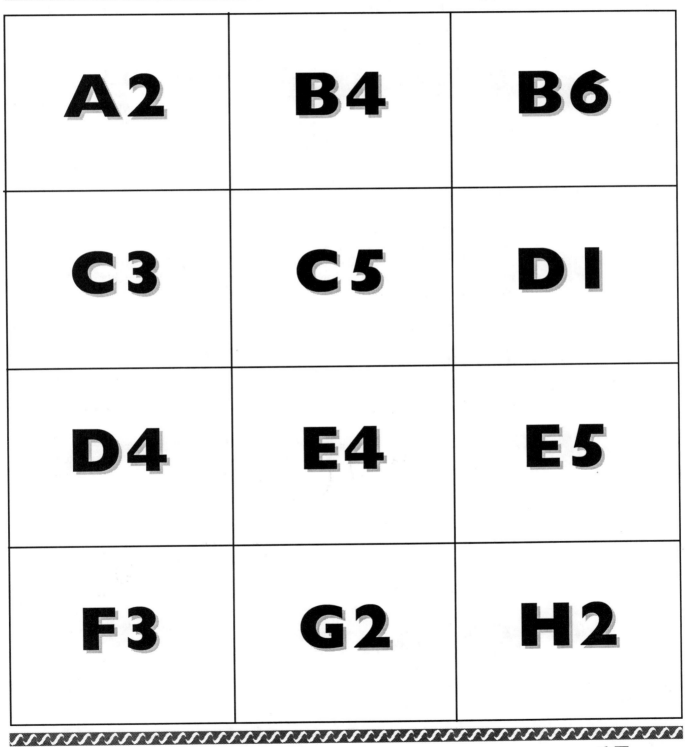

A2	**B4**	**B6**
C3	**C5**	**D1**
D4	**E4**	**E5**
F3	**G2**	**H2**

Regions of the United States

Objective:
Students will identify and explore different areas of the United States.

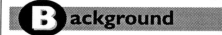

Background

Earlier the class saw how the world could be divided into geographical regions (page 35). The United States can be divided in much the same way. Regions differ not only in climate, soil, and plant and animal life but also in some cultural ways (page 53). The main regions of the U.S. are the Northwest, Northeast, Southwest, Southeast, Midwest and West Coast.

Materials

1. Reference materials.
2. United States map.
3. Tourist information (see Preparation).
4. Copies of the Airline Ticket (page 71).

For each group:

5. A copy of the Regional Study Sheet (page 70).
6. One white posterboard.
7. One 12 x 18-inch sheet of white drawing paper.
8. Markers or crayons.

Preparation

In advance, send for tourist packets from the Department of Tourism of at least one state in each region. (Lists of addresses are available from your State Department of Tourism or local library.)

Activity

Using a large map of the United States, have students identify and locate their home state. Review the function of the compass rose, and use it to help students imagine how the country might be divided into directional areas. List the six U.S. regions on the board and brainstorm a list of physical or cultural characteristics that each area might possess. Explain how cultural differences might include dress, speech patterns, and cuisine.

Next, invite students to learn more about each region by pretending to be the directors of tourism for that area. (Make sure the class understands why tourism is important to each state's economy.) Assign each small group an area and distribute the Regional Study Sheets.

Explain to the class that it is their job as tourism directors to promote their region so that people come to visit. Pass out the state tourist brochures that you have received in the mail. Let each group review the information and note what it is about the brochures that makes the region attractive to potential vacationers.

Next, direct the groups to complete the Regional Study Sheet using information from the reference materials. The groups should divide themselves into two committees. Using white poster board, Committee One will design and illustrate a travel poster depicting its region, including a caption or catchy slogan. Using white drawing paper folded lengthwise into thirds, Committee Two will design the regional brochure. Each brochure should contain interesting facts about the area, as well as illustrations. When all the groups have completed the assignment, set up each group's poster and brochure as a display. Allow the students to visit the displays.

Extension

Invite some visitors from another class, and have them pretend to be tourists planning a vacation and visiting a travel agency. Make enough copies of the Airline Ticket (page 71) for each visitor to have one. After the students have visited the displays, ask them to fill in an Airline Ticket indicating which region they would like to visit most. Collect the tickets and report the results, perhaps using a bar graph or pictograph.

Regional Study Sheet

Our region is _____ , which includes states such as

_____ , _____ , and

_____ .

1. What kinds of land forms are in your region? _____

_____

2. What kinds of water forms are in your region? _____

_____

3. What are some special places to see? _____

_____

4. What outdoor activities are available? _____

5. What cultural activities are available? (Festivals, museums, amusement parks,

concerts, etc.) _____

6. What is the climate like? _____

7. What kinds of plants and animals are there in your region? _____

_____

8. Why should anyone come to visit your region? _____

_____

Use this information to help you design your travel poster and brochure.

Airline Ticket

Atlas Airlines
Fun in the Skies

One round trip ticket to:

_____

Aisle 5   Tourist   Seat 61

State Regions

Objective:
Students will use physical and political maps to explore regions of a state.

Background

Like the United States as a whole, each state can be further divided into regions, usually based on geographical similarities alone. Physical and political maps can help students visualize these regions. A *physical map* (also called a *topographical* or *relief map*) shows the physical features of a given area by means of contour lines, colors, or raised surfaces. A *political map* shows how land is divided by the government.

Materials

1. Samples of physical and political maps.
2. Enough newspaper to cover all the desks.
3. Salt dough (see Preparation).
4. A bowl.
5. A measuring cup.
6. A spoon.

For each student:

7. A 10 x 12-inch piece of heavy cardboard (e.g., cut from the sides of boxes).
8. A sheet of bulletin board paper, large enough to completely cover the cardboard.
9. A copy of a map of your state depicting physical regions (see Preparation).

10. Scissors.
11. Glue.
12. Paper scraps.
13. Toothpicks.

Preparation

Collect the maps and prepare the pieces of cardboard.

Trace an outline of your state with the boundaries of its physical regions. Label the regions (mountains, plains, desert, etc.). Reproduce a copy for each student.

Gather the following ingredients for salt dough:
- 6 cups of salt;
- 12 cups of flour;
- 6 tablespoons of alum (available in food stores or drugstores);
- 12 cups of boiling water;
- 1 tablespoon of oil;
- A few drops each of 3 or 4 different hues of food coloring (if possible, brown, green, and blue).

Just before the lesson, start to prepare the dough by mixing the first four ingredients and leaving them to cool.

Cover the desks with newspaper.

Activity

Display a copy of a physical map and a political map. Draw a Venn diagram on the chalkboard and ask the students to compare and contrast the two types of maps (using the legend to identify colors and symbols). As students decide whether a map feature belongs to both maps or only one, write the name of the feature in the appropriate part of the diagram. Explain that sometimes a map can have both physical and political information on it.

Show the class a map of your state, and discuss the various places the students are familiar with. Point out that states can be divided into different regions, and explore those regions with the class.

Distribute the pieces of cardboard and have students cover them with the bulletin board paper. Then distribute copies of the state outline map, and have each student carefully cut out the outline and glue it to the cardboard.

While students are doing this, continue with the salt dough, adding the oil and kneading the mixture to a dough-like consistency. Divide it into batches for each region, and add appropriate food coloring to each batch (e.g., brown for mountainous areas, green for flat lands, and blue for any large bodies of water). Give each student enough of each colored dough to cover the regions on the map. Show how to pinch or smooth the dough to recreate mountains or plains. Make sure the students reserve a small piece of each dough color for the map legend. They should form these pieces into squares and place them at the bottom of map.

When the maps are completed, have students label the legend with regional names written next to the appropriate colored square. Allow the maps to dry overnight.

Extension

Before the dough fully hardens (which may take two days), have students research your state's resources and places of interest and use bits of paper to create a symbol for each. Glue the paper onto the ends of toothpicks and insert them into the proper places on the maps.

Changing Times

Objective:
Students will investigate the effects of social change.

Background

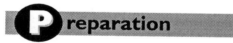

We've previously seen how natural forces such as earthquakes and volcanos can physically change the appearance of the Earth. Society, and the needs of society, can also act as agents for change.

Materials

1. Reference books (pertaining to the history of your area).
2. A copy of the Scenario Cards (page 75).

For each group:

3. A sheet of white drawing paper.
4. Crayons or markers.

Preparation

Adapt the Scenario Cards to your area. You may wish to adjust the dates as well as the contents. Make a copy of the cards and cut them apart so each small group will have one.

Activity

Share a little of your community's history with the students. If possible, show old pictures of the area and talk about how things have changed.

Review with the class the different ways that nature changes our environment and list these on the board under the heading NATURAL CHANGERS. Next write the heading HUMAN CHANGERS on the board and help students generate ideas about how people change the world around us. Remind students that America was once a wilderness. How did that change, and why? Discuss what types of change are good and what types are not so good. After listing some ideas, invite students to take a closer look at how people can bring about changes in the environment. To do this, students will write, direct, and star in a scene from the imaginary play *America*.

Give each group a Scenario Card and explain that each card describes a specific period in the history of your community. From the information on the card, groups must come up with characters and dialogue that will fit the situation. Each group member must have a part in the finished scene. Allow students time to organize and rehearse their scenes. Then have the groups present the scenes to the rest of the class in chronological order. After each performance, briefly discuss the type of change taking place and its implications for the future.

Extension

Distribute the drawing paper and have each group illustrate the scene they performed. Ask groups to write a descriptive caption at the bottom of the scene, along with the year. Assemble the pictures into an illustrated timeline and display in the classroom.

Scenario Cards

YEAR: 1561 A group of Native Americans are the first humans to arrive. They find a clearing overlooking a large body of water and decide to begin building a village.	**YEAR: 1661** Settlers from Europe need land for a new colony. The best place for a new colony, however, is occupied by a small Native American village.
YEAR: 1761 People from other parts of Europe are beginning to settle in the young town, bringing with them their own languages and customs. Those who arrive from coastal areas bring a new industry, too—shipbuilding.	**YEAR: 1861** The outbreak of the Civil War creates a great demand for ships. Many people crowd to the town in search of work.
YEAR: 1961 Other types of transportation take the place of ships (which are now mostly made of metal). Many shipbuilders have closed down, and people are out of work.	**YEAR: 2061** After years of neglect, the state government has decided to restore the town as a tourist spot in the hopes of attracting businesses to the area. The strategy works and several new businesses are started.

Taking Care of What We Have

Objective
Students will analyze different kinds of pollution and discuss ways of protecting the environment.

Background

As our population increases, so does the amount of pollution and waste we generate. Pollution is the by-product of the way we live and it affects every aspect of our lives. Helping students become aware of environmental concerns is an important step in helping to solve some of the Earth's problems.

Materials

1. Reference materials.
2. Newspapers.
3. A bag full of garbage (see Preparation).
4. A pair of plastic gloves.
5. Five sheets of white or light-colored construction paper.

For each group:

6. A copy of the Environmental Committee Study Sheet (page 78).

Preparation

Warning! This lesson is not for those with weak stomachs!

Obtain a bag of trash from the school cafeteria after a lunch period. Cover a desk surface with thick layers of newspaper for protection. Fold the pieces of construction paper lengthwise and print one of the following topics on each piece to use as committee placards:

Land   Water   Air   Noise   Other

Activity

Begin by opening a bag of garbage and setting it on top of the newspaper covered desk. Tell the students you are going to sort the items into four piles—food, plastic and metal, paper, and other (glass, wood, etc.). Wearing plastic gloves, begin to pick through the trash, asking students to decide onto which pile you should place each item.

After the bag is empty, ask students to define garbage and discuss why there is so much of it. Ask what will happen to each of the piles. Where will it go? Bring up such terms as *biodegradable* (able to break down and go back to the Earth) and *recyclable* (able to be used over and over again). Discuss which of these two categories the items in each pile fit. (Food items, wood, some metals, and most paper can be classified as biodegradable; most plastics, glass, and paper are recyclable.)

Point out to the students the amount of food that is thrown away. Ask how much of the food packaging is really necessary. Discuss other ways that the amount of garbage we produce can be reduced.

Tell students that garbage is a type of land pollution (although trash can also be found in water). Invite students to become part of a special committee that will investigate sources of pollution, and give each small group a committee placard designating their particular pollution concern. Distribute the Environmental Committee Study Sheet and direct the students to use reference materials to answer each question. Have each group assign an individual spokesperson to each question (the study sheet can be cut apart so that each member receives his or her own question). Arrange enough chairs in the front of the classroom for each committee member and have each group take turns reading questions and explaining its answers. Allow the remaining student audience to respond to the committee remarks and ask questions. Continue until all the committees have shared.

Extensions

- Talk about the different "Pollution Solutions" each committee discussed. Discuss and select a pollution project the class may want to take on for the remainder of the school year. Projects could range from simply picking up playground trash once a week to a more ambitious school-wide recycling program. (The books listed in the Bibliography at the end of the book can provide you with more ideas.)
- Use the Its in the Can! Bulletin Board on page 106 to round out this activity.

Name ______________________________

Environmental Sheet

We are assigned ______________________

______________________________ pollution.

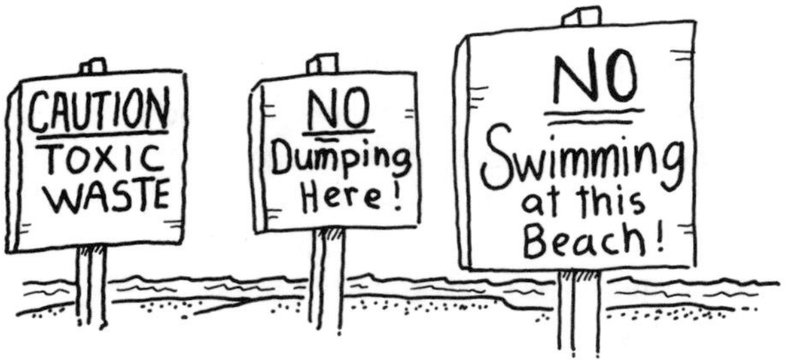

1. What does this mean? ______________________________

____

2. How does it happen? ______________________________

____

3. What causes it? ______________________________

____

4. What problems does it cause? ______________________________

____

5. Whom does it affect? ______________________________

____

6. What can we do about it? ______________________________

____

____

____

____

____

____

____

____

Finally...

As a fun end-of-unit activity, have students show what they know by preparing a special presentation. Remind the class of their space "alter egos." Tell them that their Earth "field trip" is now at an end and they must complete a report detailing what they have learned. Set time aside for them to prepare a group report, complete with visuals. Each group should decide what the report will cover and who will write (or draw) each section. On presentation day, encourage students to come dressed as their space alter ego. (You might want to provide a few out-of-this-world refreshments as well!)

Bulletin Boards

About This Section

The bulletin board projects described here are divided into two sections—Reinforcement and For Further Study. The Reinforcement bulletin boards do just that—reinforce a concept currently being studied. The Further Study boards invite students to investigate a new topic related to one of the lesson concepts.

You will probably find it most convenient to prepare a bulletin board in advance and then allot several minutes at the end of a lesson for students to work at the project.

Each project description includes patterns for the items used on the boards.

For virtually all of the projects you will need the following materials:

1. A stapler;
2. Letter stencils;
3. A paintbrush;
4. Poster paints;
5. A sheet of bulletin board paper;
6. A 5 x 9-inch card;
7. A black marker;
8. An 8 x 10-inch manila envelope;
9. Sets of hook-sided and loop-sided velcro tabs (available from sewing stores) for some of the bulletin boards.

Any other material needed are listed with the individual project.

Reinforcement Bulletin Boards

Buried Treasure

Directions

1. Make the heading "Buried Treasure" (either freehand or with letter stencils) and attach it at the top end of the board.

2. Enlarge the treasure chest on page 86, make three copies, and label each as shown above. (The coin beside the chest can be copied as a decoration.) Cut slits as indicated by dashed lines and staple the chests to the board.

3. Reproduce four copies each of the three types of "booty" on page 87 and print one of the following question ends on the front of each piece. Write the answers (shown in parentheses) on the back.

   • The adventures of Caribbean pirates? (Encyclopedia)

   • The location of Captiva Island? (Atlas)

   • How a bar of gold is made? (Encyclopedia)

   • What the word "bullion" means? (Dictionary)

   • Information on the pirate flag, the Jolly Roger? (Encyclopedia)

   • In what ocean the Bahama Islands are located? (Atlas)

   • How to spell "galleon"? (Dictionary)

   • Different types of precious gems? (Encyclopedia)

   • Whether "buccaneer" is a noun or verb? (Dictionary)

   • How far the Orinoco River is from the Isthmus of Panama in the Spanish Main? (Atlas)

   • Types of treasures that have been found? (Encyclopedia)

• Synonyms for the word "pirate"?
  (Dictionary)

4. Print these directions on a 5 x 9-inch index card:

Ahoy, Mates! Dictionaries, encyclopedias, and atlases are important tools that help us locate information quickly. Test your knowledge of these reference materials. Take the pieces of pirate "loot" from the envelope. Read each piece and put it in the correct chest. When you are through, check your answers by looking at the back of each piece.

5. Write "Where would you find...?" on the front of a manila envelope. Store the directions card and the pirate "loot" in the envelope and secure it to the front of the board.

Buried Treasure Patterns

Buried Treasure
Patterns (cont.)

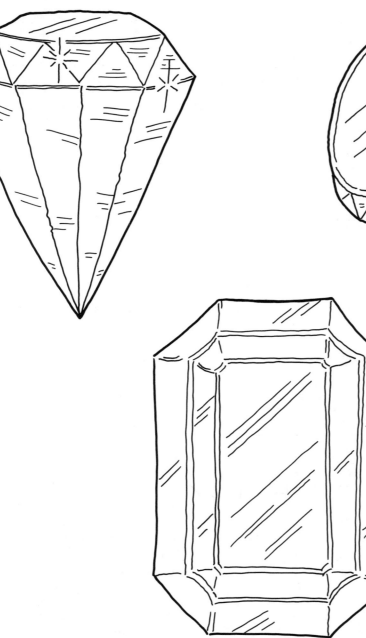

Feature Presentation

Topic:
Reinforcing the identification of physical features—land, water, and human-made.

Materials

1. Black and yellow construction paper.
2. White posterboard.

Directions

1. Cover the board with black construction paper.
2. Use letter stencils and bulletin board paper to make the heading "Feature Presentation" and staple it to the board. Make marquee lights out of yellow circles for the border.
3. Enlarge and cut out three popcorn boxes (page 89), labeling each as shown above. Attach the boxes to the board, leaving the tops open.
4. Using the pattern on page 89, trace 12 popcorn pieces on white posterboard and cut them out. On the front of each piece, print one of the following movie titles. On the back, write the answer (shown in parentheses below).
   • Airport (Manufactured)
   • Desert Song (Land)
   • A Bridge Too Far (Manufactured)
   • The Plainsman (Land)
   • River of No Return (Water)
   • 42nd Street (Manufactured)
   • How Green Was My Valley (Land)
   • South Pacific (Water)
   • Summer School (Manufactured)
   • The Big Store (Manufactured)
   • Home Alone (Manufactured)
   • Jurassic Park (Land)
5. Write the following directions on a 5 x 9-inch index card:

   Welcome to today's feature presentation! Land, water, and manufactured features can all be found on the Earth's surface. Read each piece of popcorn and see if you can find the type of feature "hidden" in each movie title. Then put the popcorn into the right box. Check your answers when you are through by looking on the back of each piece.
6. Place the directions card and popcorn pieces in a manila envelope and secure it to the front of the board.

Feature
Presentation Patterns

Hats Off!

Materials

1. Ten pairs of hook-sided and loop-sided velcro tabs.

Directions

1. Using brown poster paint, paint two hat racks on bulletin board paper and attach them to the board. Label them as shown. Attach hook-sided velcro tabs to each hat rest.
2. Use letter stencils to make the heading "Hats Off" and staple it to the board.
3. Enlarge each of the hats (page 91) and place loop-sided velcro on the back of each.
4. Write these directions on a 5 x 9-inch index card:

Hats off to those people who help make our lives better! Human resources can be divided into two groups: those who produce or sell something (a *good*) and those who offer a *service*. Read each hat and decide whether it belongs on the goods hat rack or the service hat rack. Check your answers when you are through by looking at the back of this card.

5. On the back of the card write these answers:
Service: Doctor, Firefighter, Police Officer, Sailor, Professor.
Good: Chef, Artist, Farmer, Construction Worker, Miner.
6. Store the directions card and the hats in a manila envelope and secure it to the front of the board.

Hats Off! Patterns

All-Star Game

Topic:
Reinforcing the use of a grid.

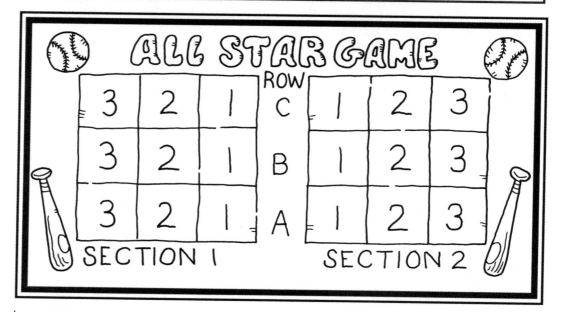

ALL STAR GAME

3	2	1	ROW	1	2	3
3	2	1	C	1	2	3
3	2	1	B	1	2	3
3	2	1	A	1	2	3

SECTION 1   SECTION 2

Materials

1. Eighteen pairs of hook-sided and loop-sided velcro.

Directions

1. Use letter stencils to create the "All-Star Game" heading.
2. Copy the stadium sections onto bulletin board paper using black marker. In each seat square, attach a tab of hook-sided velcro.
3. Reproduce 18 baseball caps (from page 93). On each cap, write the name of a major league baseball team and place a tab of loop-sided velcro on the back. Decide which hat will go in which seat.
4. Reproduce 18 tickets (from page 93), nine for Section 1 and nine for Section 2. On each ticket, write a team name and the corresponding seat coordinates for that team's cap.
5. On a 5 x 9-inch index card, write these directions:

    Let's play ball! See how well you can find the right seat for each baseball fan. Read the team on each cap and find the matching ticket. Use the Section, Row, and Seat coordinates to put that cap in the correct place. To check your work, turn this card over.
6. Cut out the Answer Key (from page 93), fill in the answers, and glue it to the back of the card.
7. Store the directions card and caps in a manila envelope and secure it to the board.

All-Star Game Patterns

Answer Key

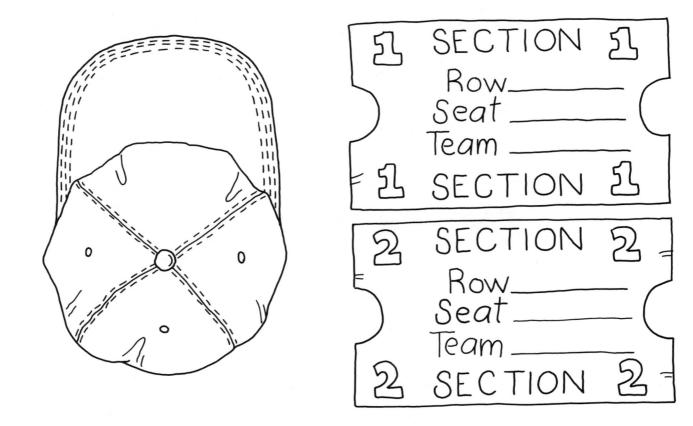

SECTION 1 1
Row _____
Seat _____
Team _____
1 SECTION 1

2 SECTION 2
Row _____
Seat _____
Team _____
2 SECTION 2

Land of Make-Believe

Materials

1. Colored markers, crayons, or water colors.
2. Seven pairs of hook-sided and loop-sided velcro.
3. Tag board.
4. A brad fastener.

Background

1. Copy the map of the Land of Make-Believe onto a white-paper-covered bulletin board. Use black marker for the outline and color in with markers, crayons, or watercolors. Attach hook-sided velcro to each location on the map and label as shown.
2. Make the compass rose spinner by cutting a large circle out of tag board and dividing it into four parts. Mark each part NW, NE, SE, and SW. Cut a pointer out of different colored tag board and secure loosely to the center of the circle with a brad fastener. Staple the spinner to the center of the board.
3. Reproduce each of the Make-Believe characters. Color, cut out, and mount them on tag board. Attach loop-sided velcro to the back of each figure.
4. Print these directions on a 5 x 9-inch index card:

   Welcome to the land of Make-Believe! Remove all of the residents of Make-Believe from the envelope. Now spin the spinner to find which direction to put them in. (If you get the same direction more than twice, spin again until you've covered all the locations.) When you are through, write a short story about the characters and where they are on the map.
5. Store the Directions card and figures in a manila envelope and secure it to the front of the board.

Land of Make-Believe Patterns

For Further Study Bulletin Boards

What's in a Name?

Topic:
Discovering some unusual fields of scientific study.

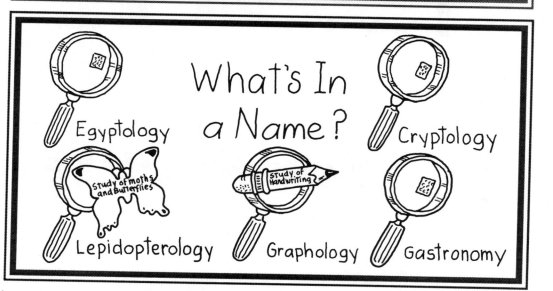

What's In a Name?

Egyptology

Cryptology

Study of moths and Butterflies

Study of Handwriting

Lepidopterology

Graphology

Gastronomy

Materials

1. Five pairs of hook-sided and loop-sided velcro.

Background

1. Use letter stencils to create the heading "What's in a Name?" and staple it to the board.

2. Enlarge, color, and cut out five magnifying glasses from page 100. Attach hook-sided velcro to the front of each. Attach the glasses to the board and label as shown above.

3. Enlarge, color and cut out the picture patterns. Carefully print these definitions on the appropriate picture:

- On the butterfly: The study of butterflies and moths.

- On the mummy: The study of things Egyptian.
- On the pencil: The study of handwriting.
- On the trenchcoat: The study of secret writing.
- On the plate: The science of good eating.

4. Attach loop-sided velcro to the back of each picture.

5. Print these directions on a 5 x 9-inch card:

You may know that geography is the study of the Earth. You may also know that biology looks at the human body. But did you know that chromatology is the science of colors or that pedology is the study of children?

Under each magnifying glass is the name of a special science. Try your skill at matching these definitions to the correct glass. When you are finished, check your answers by looking at the back of this card.

6. On the back of the card write:
   - Lepidopterology: The study of butterflies and moths.
   - Egyptology: The study of things Egyptian.
   - Graphology: The study of handwriting.
   - Cryptology: The study of secret writing.
   - Gastronomy: The science of good eating.

7. Store the directions card and pictures in a manila envelope and secure it to the front of the board.

What's in a Name? Patterns

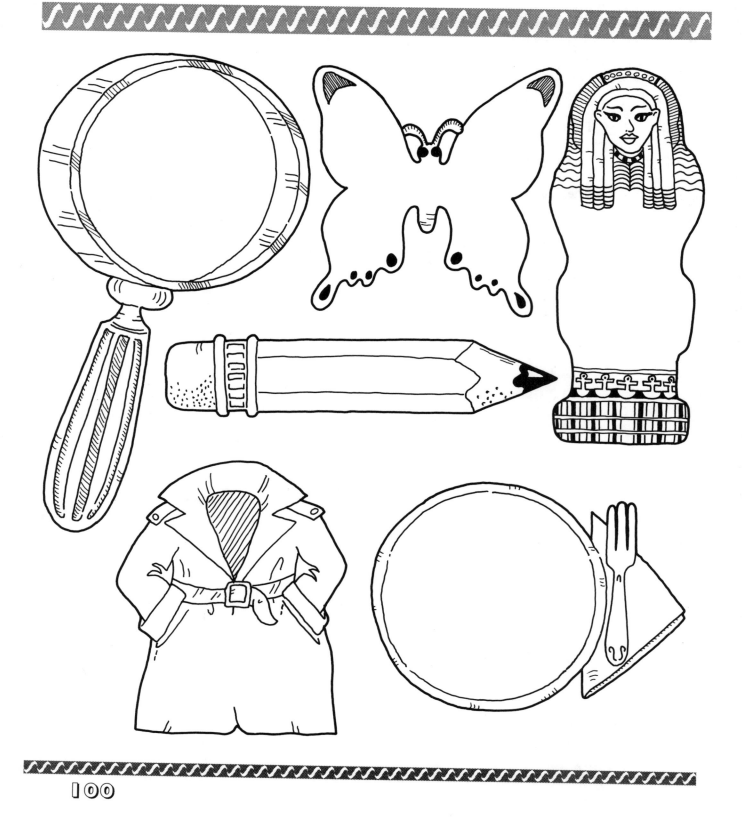

How's the Weather?

Topic:
Exploring different types of maps and weather conditions.

Materials

1. Clear contact paper.
2. Tagboard.
3. Damp paper towels.

Directions

1. Use letter stencils to make the heading "How's the Weather?" and staple to the front of the board.
2. Copy the map and weather symbols onto bulletin board paper using black marker. Attach the paper to the board. Cover the map portion of the paper with clear contact paper.
3. Copy and cut apart the Forecast cards (page 102). Mount them on tagboard.
4. Print these directions on a 5 x 9-inch index card:

   Have you ever wanted to be a TV weatherperson? Now's your chance! On the board is an outline map of the United States. On each side of the map, you'll see some special symbols. Meteorologists use these symbols to explain what's happening with the weather.

   Pick a weather forecast card and use the black marker to draw the symbols where they belong. (Example: If it's raining in the Northeast, draw straight lines on that part of the map.) Remember to use the compass rose for directional help.

   When you are finished, wipe the board clean with a damp paper towel. Try writing and then drawing your own forecast!
5. Store the directions card and washable black marker in a manila envelope and secure it to the front of the board. Have one or two damp paper towels available.

How's the Weather?
Forecast Cards

SUMMER

The maximum temperature in the Northeast is 70 degrees. There is drizzle over the Northwest. There are clear skies over much of the South.

WINTER

There is snow in the North. The maximum temperature in the East is 45 degrees. It is cloudy in the South. It is drizzling in the West.

SPRING

There are partly cloudy skies over the West Coast. There is moderate rain over much of the South. It is very foggy in the North. There are showers in the East.

FALL

There is heavy fog over the Northwest. There is a hurricane over the Gulf of Mexico in the South. There is moderate rain in the East.

Games Around the World

Topic:
Appreciating the cultures of other peoples through their games.

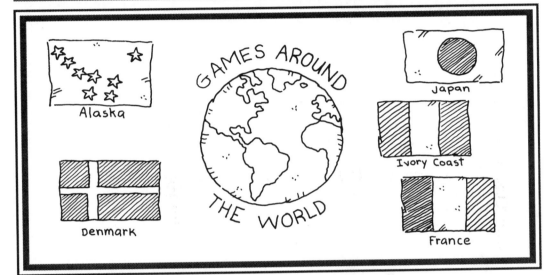

Materials

1. A sheet of white construction paper.
2. Pushpins.
3. A 36-inch length of string tied in a loop.

Directions

1. Cut a large circle out of the construction paper and paint it to resemble the Earth. Use letter stencils to make the heading "Games Around The World" and staple it to the board as shown above.
2. Enlarge each flag on page 105 and color them accordingly:
   Alaska—yellow stars on blue background.
   Denmark—white cross on red background.
   France—blue, white, and red stripes.
   Ivory Coast—red, white, and green stripes.
   Japan—red circle on white backgound
3. On the back of each flag, write the directions for the appropriate game:
   • **Catch Your Tail (Ivory Coast and other parts of Africa):**
      Divide into five teams. Team members hold each other's hands. The last person in line has a scarf stuffed in a back pocket or tied loosely around the waist. Each team tries to grab the scarf (tail) of another team.
   • **Finger Count-Off (France)**
      A leader counts to three. When three is called, everyone holds up as many fingers as they choose, and at the same time shouts out a guess as to

the total number of fingers being held up. The leader counts the number of fingers and the one who comes closest wins and becomes the new leader.

- **Jan Ken Po (Japan):**

You'll know this game—but did you know it was popular in Japan?

Divide into pairs. Each player counts to three by pounding a fist against the palm of the other hand. When three is called, each partner must form scissors, paper, or stone with one hand. The winner is declared by these rules—scissors cut paper, paper smothers stone, or stone breaks scissors.

To form Jan (scissors) extend your middle and index finger. To form Ken (paper) hold your hand out flat. To form Po (stone) clench your fist.

- **The Bear (Denmark)**

One person is named "It." As soon as It tags someone, they join hands and chant "The bear is coming!" Then they try to tag others with their free hands. Every time someone is tagged, he or she joins hands and becomes part of the bear.

- **Ear Pull (Alaska)**

Divide into pairs and sit facing each other. A loop of string is hooked around one ear of each pair. Pairs must pull against the string, using only their heads, until it slips off an ear. The one with the string remaining is the winner.

4. Attach the flags to the board with a pushpin.

5. Set aside some time to play each of these games or allow students to remove the flags and take them out during recess to play.

Games Around the
World Patterns

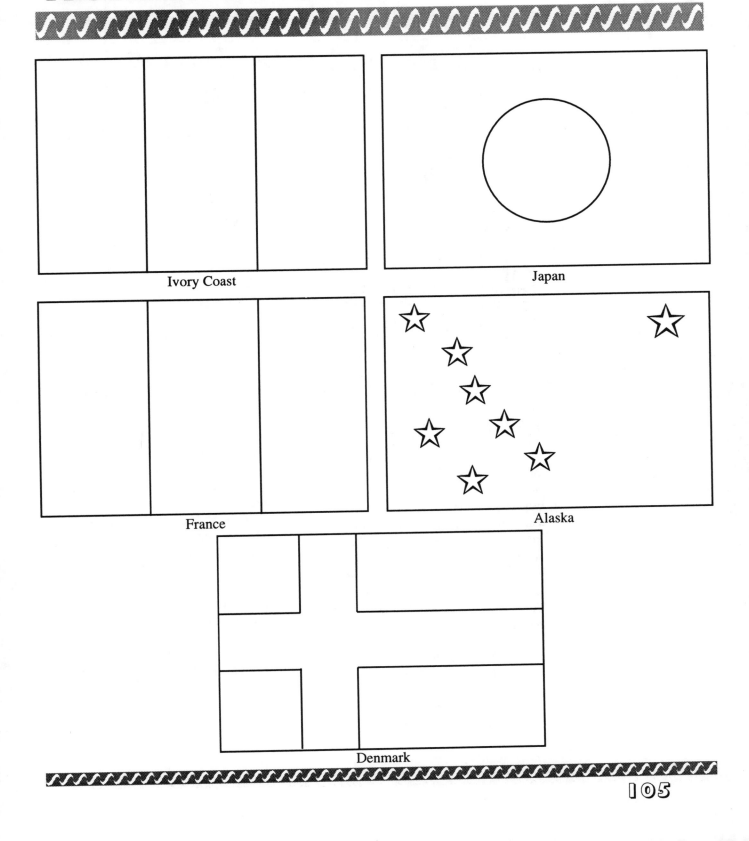

Ivory Coast

Japan

France

Alaska

Denmark

It's in the Can!

Topic:
Classifying different sources of pollution.

Directions

1. Use letter stencils to make the heading "It's In The Can!" and attach it to the board.
2. Enlarge and make four gray trash cans, labeled as shown above. Staple each one to the board, leaving the top of each can open.
3. Enlarge each of the pieces of "trash" on page 107 and write one of the following answers on the back of each piece:
   • Water (oil drop)
   • Other: Noise (radio)
   • Land (diaper)
   • Air (cigarette)
   • Other: Noise (jet)
   • Other: Ozone (aerosol can)
   • Air (car)
   • Land (can)
   • Air (smokestack)
   • Land (tire)
   • Water (sewage pipe)
   • Water (detergent bubbles)
4. Print these directions on a 5 x 9-inch card:

   What kinds of pollution are there? What are some of the things that cause each kind of pollution? Knowing the answers is one of the first steps toward solving this worldwide problem.

   Each of these trash cans has one type of pollution written on it. Look at the pieces of "trash" and decide which can it belongs in. When you are through, check your work by looking on the back of each piece.
5. Store the directions card and trash pieces in a manila envelope and secure it to the front of the board.

It's in the Can! Patterns

Car Exhaust
(air)

Oil (water)

(water)

Detergents
(water)

Jet
(other-noise)

Aerosol Cans
(other-ozone)

Tire
(land)

Radio
(other-noise)

Smoke Stacks
(air)

Diaper
(land)

Cigarette Smoke
(air)

Sewage
(water)

Bibliography

Cooperative Learning: Getting Started, by Susan Ellis and Susan Whalen, New York: Scholastic, Inc., 1990.

Disaster! Series, Chicago: Children's Press, 1982.

Earth, the Ever-Changing Planet, by Donald M. Silver, New York: Random House, 1989.

50 Simple Things Kids Can Do to Save the Earth, by John Javna, Kansas City: Andrews and McMeel, 1990.

Garbage, by Maria Fleming, New York: Scholastic, 1992.

Geography From A–Z, by Jack Knowlton, New York: Thomas Y. Crowell, 1988.

The Kid's World Almanac of the United States, by Thomas G. Aylesworth, New York: Pharos Books, 1990.

Landmasses: Fun, Facts and Activities, by Caroline Arnold, New York: Watts, 1985.

Let's Discover What People Do, Milwaukee: Raintree Publishers, 1981.

Look Inside the Earth, by Gina Ingoglia, New York: Grosset and Dunlap, 1991.

Maps and Globes, by David Lambert, New York: Bookwright Press, 1987.

Our Amazing Ocean, by David A. Adler, Mahwah, New Jersey: Troll Associates, 1983.

Our Endangered Earth Series: Land Animals, by David Cook, New York: Crown Books, 1983.

Our Population: The Changing Face of America, by Charles B. Nam, New York: Walker & Co., 1988.

Our World Pollution and Conservation, Morristown, New Jersey: Silver Burdett, 1988.

The Usborne Book of Earth Facts, by Lynn Bresler, Tulsa: Usborne Publishing, 1986.

The Viking Children's World Atlas, by Jacqueline Tivers and Michael Day, New York: Puffin Books, 1986.

Young Students World Atlas, Chicago: Rand McNally, 1982.

Notes

Notes

Notes